HOPE  KNOWS

BEYOND THE
PAST

elaine starner

JPV PRESS

Author photo: Denice Rovira Hazlett at Sprouted Acorn Photography

Author can be reached at P.O. Box 185, Walnut Creek, OH 44687, or by email at *myhopeknows@gmail.com.*

All other external material referenced has been used by permission.

Printed in the United States of America

First Printing, 2018

ISBN 978-1-946389-08-4

JPV 🔥 PRESS

2106 Main Street / PO Box 201
Winesburg, OH 44690

www.jpvpress.com

For Rosie.
Thank you for
encouraging me.

CONTENTS

PRAYER FOR THE PRISONER:

*Listen to my cry, for I am in
desperate need. Set me free
from my prison.*

– **from PSALM 142:6, 7** NIV –

FREEDOM FOR PRISONERS

THE MISSION

I've been sent to set prisoners free, to proclaim that captives will be released!

- LUKE 4:18 AP -

Everyone in our group felt the ominous chill that settled over us. The cold-gray, sprawling old complex had been a prison where men lived in cells that were more like cages, smaller than my apartment bedroom. The cages were stacked several stories high. No sunshine broke the gloom.

As we walked through each wing and listened to our guide's explanations, I was conscious of bars, locks, and chains everywhere.

How could those who lived here for any amount of time hold onto hope for a life someday outside the unyielding, dirty stone walls? Could they even remember what freedom was like?

Thoughts about those prisoners and what their days must have been like lingered with me for many weeks after we had finished the tour of the old prison.

How many prisoners, just as hopeless, wander our world today? They may walk through their days freely, but they are wearing shackles forged by many things.

The apostle Peter wrote that "you are a slave to whatever controls you" (2 Peter 2:19).

Maybe at this point, you're objecting: "Not me. I am not a prisoner or a slave. I'm not sitting in a dungeon."

But consider Peter's statement. What does control you? What dictates your day's schedule or dominates your thoughts? Do you feel helpless in the face of certain things in your life? Are there forces controlling your days and stifling the life in you?

Many dark things can hold us captive. Even "good" things can be our prison. External forces or events might control us, but more often it's our own choices that land us in a hostile country, slaves to a power that opposes and hinders God's good plan for our lives.

Jesus said that He came to the world and into our lives to break our chains and bring us out of dark dungeons into a new life. There is good news for anyone who is:

> tyrannized by a guilty conscience or
>   others' expectations
> locked into patterns of negative thinking
> shackled by grief
> driven by anger or bitterness
> paralyzed by fear
> bound by chains of addiction
> enslaved by human nature
> fettered by past hurts
> oppressed by human or spiritual enemies
> living in fear of dying and eternal
>   punishment for wrongs

In one of the descriptions above, do you recognize your own chains or the bars of your prison cell?

Whatever your dungeon is, keep it in mind as we listen to Jesus' promise that He comes to set prisoners free.

He comes to rescue all who suffer in dungeons

where darkness, fear, guilt, pain, distrust, or disbelief squash hope and smother light and shrivel life.

He can free everyone who is trapped, addicted, bound, enslaved... or just plain stuck.

He comes to break the chains we drag along through life, chains that control us and restrict our living.

There *is* hope for every prisoner and everyone who is held captive.

 "LORD, HELP!"

"LORD, help!" they cried in their trouble, and he saved them from their distress.

– PSALM 107:13 –

Facing those things that keep us enslaved is painful. Yet I'm guessing it might be why you picked up this book. It is the reason I wrote this book. I needed the freedom Jesus promised He could give, and I needed to know how to find it.

Psalm 107 outlines many of our stories. If you take time to read the chapter thoughtfully, you might recognize yourself. My own story is there, and I wouldn't be surprised if you find yours, too.

Verses 4-9 describe those who wandered in a wilderness, lost, homeless, and starving. Do you know that feeling? Many of us have wandered in a wilderness of grief, abuse, loss, and distress, and felt as though life was slipping away.

The Psalm continues: Then those wanderers called out for God's help, and He rescued them. He "led them straight to safety, to a city where they could live," and He satisfied their hunger and thirst. After starving in the wilderness with no hope for your life, can you imagine finally settling into a place where you are safe and your longings are satisfied?

Seven more verses (10-16) tell about prisoners sitting in "darkness and deepest gloom, imprisoned in iron chains of misery." They landed there through their own choices, yet when they called out to God for help, "he snapped their chains and... broke down their prison gates of bronze; he cut apart their bars of iron."

Their own foolish choices landed them in prisons of misery. Finally, they called out to God for help.

His answer?

Again, rescue!

We, too, often land in bondage through our own foolish choices, but He has the power to break that oppression. Not only does He have the power, but He is waiting, wanting us to call on His help.

God wants to bring us out of darkness and give us joy and great, expectant hope. He wants to break our chains and set us free to live. He wants to rescue us from wandering in the wilderness and give us a place of safety and vitality. This has been the Creator's character and His promise from the beginning of our time.

The question is: Will we call out to Him for help?

Generations before Jesus lived on earth, David knew God's power; he wrote again and again in the psalms that the Lord "sets the prisoners free and gives them joy" (Psalm 68:6).

David had learned that God did indeed hear and respond to the cries of those in chains and shackles, those imprisoned, those wandering in the wilderness.

God meant for His creation to live in joyful freedom. But when the human race chose to go its own way, it turned from God and walked right into slavery to many other things.

Yet the Creator, in great love and compassion for us, still comes to the rescue. He still offers us freedom and joy.

Our stories can also read: *They called out to God for help, and He rescued them*

 THE GOD WHO RESCUES

He gave his life to purchase freedom for everyone. This is
the message God gave to the world at just the right time.
- 1 TIMOTHY 2:6 -

Jesus came to earth on a mission. He knew where the mission would take him—right to the heart of the enemy's kingdom. That enemy was bent on slavery and destruction of human lives, and Jesus' mission was to swing open doors of jail cells and renew those lives.

And so He became a human being just like us. He lived as part of a family and a neighborhood, and he had cousins, aunts, uncles, and childhood friends. He learned a trade and went to the synagogue and studied the Jewish traditions and laws, preparing to be a teacher.

"I've come to declare freedom and set captives free!" Those were some of His first public words about His mission in the world.

Yet carrying out this mission would cost Him dearly, because He had purposely walked into the kingdom of darkness where the devil rules—an enemy whose one goal is to ruin God's plans.

And in the end, this man accepted humiliation and ridicule, was despised, tortured, and eventually killed because He was devoted to the mission of setting people free so they could live the life God intended to give us at the beginning.

He was God, yet He was willing to live as a human and bear all of that suffering to buy us back from our slavery and the darkness that holds us.

God would do that for us? Even though we don't deserve it?

Yes. He loves His creation that much. He did it so we could live in freedom.

This is the good news—He is the God who rescues and saves. That's the entire story of the Bible and of the relationship between God and His creation.

STILL ALIVE, STILL CARRYING OUT THE MISSION

For the Lord is the Spirit, and wherever the Spirit of the Lord is, there is freedom.

– 2 CORINTHIANS 3:17 –

Christ paid the ransom—He died a horrible death to give us freedom from all that enslaves us and robs us of life. (Remember what you have identified as your own dungeon or chains?)

But Christ's death was not the end of the story. It was only the beginning.

He did not stay in the grave.

I know this is the point where many people have difficulty believing, but this is also the key to all of Christian hope. If Jesus' death would have been the end, then indeed there is little hope for us because we're building our lives on foolish stories.

But Jesus was given new life.

He is alive today, and He leads the way, showing that God's power is supreme. He has established a kingdom now, within human history, and He is all about rescuing those who believe in Him. He is freeing them from other forces so they can live in a new way—the way of His Kingdom, modeled by His own life and teaching. It's the way God meant for us to live when He first created humans.

Jesus has the power to rescue us. His power works to break whatever chains and prison bars hold us captive. That's His mission. That's what He comes to our lives to do.

Now, at this very time when people say gloomily that everything in the world looks hopeless, Jesus is alive and still carrying out His mission on this earth.

"LET'S BE REALISTIC"

We also know that the Son did not come to help angels; he came to help the descendants of Abraham.

- HEBREWS 2:16 -

"That all sounds wonderful," you might say, "but let's be realistic. No one can fix the mess I'm in. No one can break this fear and anxiety I live with. No one can set me free from the awful guilt I carry. No one can heal the deep wounds in my life."

Freedom from whatever holds you prisoner may seem an impossible dream. And the truth is, freedom is impossible—unless the power of Christ works wonders in our lives.

If we say, "Let's be realistic," shall we talk of the world's *realistic* or of God's *realistic?* There is a difference, you know.

What is God's truth? We need to know, because it is only what He says is true that can give us hope.

Let's look at what *hope* really is.

Unfortunately, in our daily conversations, the word has taken on a meaning that is not what God means when He says He is the God of all hope. When we use the word, it is often the equivalent of a *wish*. We *hope* our team wins. I *hope* to lose ten pounds this summer. We *hope* that we are not disturbing someone.

But the word *hope* used by God in the Scriptures—His direct Word to us—is more than a wish. The hope God gives is something we can be certain of; hope knows that what He has promised *will happen,* and He does not lie or renege on His promises. Hope knows this, and looks forward to the fulfillment of the promise, knowing it will come.

Think of hope as a bridge God has laid before us on our journey. It carries us over rough patches in the road, or through places we see as daunting and impassable. Even though we often cannot see where the bridge ends and the road goes onward, we trust the bridge to carry us and enable us to move forward.

God's promise that He can free prisoners is a bridge of hope that allows us to look ahead, to live with great expectation, because we know we can walk out of our dungeons and leave our chains behind. We're no longer bound and paralyzed.

As our opening Scripture says, Jesus came to help us. We needed His help. If we could have worked out our freedom on our own, there would have been no need for Him to come to earth on a rescue mission. There would be no need for Him to be saying to you today, "I will set you free from your prison."

But we cannot work it out on our own. (Think of your own dungeon or chains.) All of us know that—we've tried, we've failed, and we still drag around our chains.

If Jesus does not have the power to free us from our prisons, then His mission has failed. And all other hopes are futile.

But the hope that is sure is this: Christ *does* have the power to rescue us and set us free.

This is what God says is reality: He is the God of great wonders and the God of all hope. He is alive, and He can break our chains and free us from our prisons. He gives us that bridge of promise so that we can walk ahead with confidence.

THE REWARD FOR TRUSTING

The reward for trusting him will be the salvation of your souls.
- **1 PETER 1:9** *-*

Jesus says, "I came to rescue you. To get you out of chains and give you a life with all the privileges of a child of God. Trust me. Let me give you that life. I have the power to do it."

Each one of us knows what shackles restrict our living. What might our lives look like if those chains were broken? What if we could walk away from the slavery or walk out of our jail cell—a free person?

Christ promises that freedom to those who trust Him to do what He says He can do.

The apostle Peter wrote a letter reminding Christians: You have a choice. Even though you can't *see* Christ, you can choose to trust Him. And if you choose to trust Him, "the reward for trusting him will be the salvation of your souls" (1 Peter 1:9).

Did you know that the word *salvation* means *rescue?* Peter goes on to say that this salvation/ rescue is such exciting stuff that even the angels eagerly watch the unfolding of God's plan to rescue people (see 1 Peter 1:12).

That word is for us, today. Christ came to rescue us from hopeless lives. He came to move us from the kingdom of darkness to His kingdom of light. We have the choice. If we choose to seek Him, trust Him, and believe in His power, exciting things await. Even the angels are excited about what God is doing.

This is not just a promise for some far-off day; it is a promise for life here and now. His mission is still to smash our shackles. Jesus the Rescuer comes into our lives to free us from things that restrain us, immobilize us, and control us. He comes to break all other powers and release us to live new lives.

Whatever it was that you identified as your dungeon or your chains—trusting Jesus will result in the rescue of your heart, soul, mind, and life.

I cannot tell you specifics of how He will bring freedom to your life, but I can tell you that He will. It is the reason He came to earth. It is His mission today.

He is the Rescuer. We can trust Him to do what He said He will do.

THE GOD OF ALL HOPE

Live with great expectation. Be truly glad. There is wonderful joy ahead!
- from 1 PETER 1:3, 6 -

In this book of meditations, we want to look specifically at how our past can hold us prisoner and then see the wonderful things God does to rescue us.

Might you and I be among those who sit in dark dungeons of our own creation? Are we chained by guilt and shame arising from our past? Have we said and done things that we know can never be undone? Have we broken things that can never be mended? Did we go down paths that brought harm and chaos not only to our own lives but also to the lives of those around us?

Most of us have made a mess of things at one time or another, and we've wondered if we must carry our blame and remorse for the rest of our lives. Will we forever be prisoners of our past?

How can there be any hope for our past?

What does God say about our past?

What can our hope know?

We may feel as though there's no way to "fix" our lives. What's done is done and can't be undone. We've made bad decisions. We've done terrible things. We've lived only for ourselves. Maybe we've even told God, "I know this is wrong, but I don't care." You can add all the specifics of your own story, but everyone who wears chains of the past wonders, *Is there any hope for my life?*

We have many pages still in this book, but I'll tell you the end of the story, something my hope knows: *Live with great expectation. There is wonderful joy ahead!*

Here are two helps for you as you read these meditations.

At the beginning of each section, you'll find a Psalm prayer. Most of these were written by David, a man with an unusual and intense relationship with God. His life was filled with much trouble and turmoil. He, too, had a "past," regrets, and guilt. You'll recognize many of David's thoughts and feeling as very much like things you've felt and thought yourself.

The prayers for each section are short and easy to memorize. Use them as your own prayers when appropriate. For example, the prayer for this section says (in my words), "I am desperate, Lord. Set me free from my prison."

The second help you'll find is an appendix at the back of the book with many more Scriptures that give you assurance of the hope we're thinking about in each section. If you want to hear much more of what God says about each subject, dig into those Scriptures.

What you read there is God's reality, His answers to our questions.

For more promises of freedom,
see the appendix for a list of additional Scriptures.

PRAYER FOR THOSE WHO HAVE A PAST:

LORD, if you kept a record of our sins,

who, O Lord, could ever survive?

But you offer forgiveness.

I am counting on [you], LORD.

I have put my hope in [your] word.

– from PSALM 130:3-5 –

FREE FROM
THE PENALTY

 **"JOY!"**

Oh what joy for those whose disobedience is forgiven,
whose sin is put out of sight! Yes, what joy for those whose
record the LORD has cleared of guilt.

- from PSALM 32:1-2 -

"I can never forgive myself!"

Have you said that? Or thought it?

A great, exhausting burden of guilt and grief crushes the life out of us. We have done the unforgivable, cracked apart the lives of everyone close to us, and—like Humpty Dumpty in hundreds of shattered pieces—we are sure that nothing will ever put things back together again.

We can see no sliver of light, no hope that life will ever be good again. And we have done that not only to ourselves, but to those we love. We don't deserve the forgiveness of anyone, and we know it.

But there is good news.

The good news is this: God's truth is that He really will forgive us for whatever we have done. Jesus really did pay the price for all of our wrongs and failures—even the most terrible things.

And there will be joy for those whose record the Lord has cleared.

Joy? There's a possibility of joy?

When I'm hounded by my guilty conscience?

When I still carry old grudges?

When I have so much trouble controlling my temper?

Joy?

Even though I'm an alcoholic?

When I am haunted by the way I cheated my boss?

When I've done such terrible things that my relationships are all in shambles?

Yes. There can be joy!

The joy comes once we begin to grasp and

believe this hope—even though we cannot imagine how it can be—that God clears the record of all our guilt.

Ask the Father for this hope. Because this is the hope that deals with my past and with your past.

The guilt of the past can be gone. We can walk out of that prison and live with joy.

 "KINDNESS"

He is so rich in kindness and grace that he purchased our freedom with the blood of his Son and forgave our sins.
- EPHESIANS 1:7 -

For God chose to save us through our Lord Jesus Christ, not to pour out his anger on us.
- 1 THESSALONIANS 5:9 -

What if we find this hope—a hope that our record is cleared—impossible to believe? What if we've made such a mess of things that we know we can never be forgiven? What if whispers keep reminding us of past actions? What if we know all too well that dark places still lurk within us? What if we don't deserve to be forgiven?

We don't deserve it.

We've openly rebelled against our Creator. We have intentionally left God's path and stubbornly set ourselves against Him. Even with a change of heart, we can never be "good enough" to wipe the slate clean and deserve Christ's rescue.

Human thinking tells us that we must pay for our wrongs. It's the way this world works—you break the law, you pay the penalty. But there is something at work that goes beyond this world's thinking... and this "something" gives us hope.

It is God's kindness.

This hope has nothing to do with what we deserve. It is all about God's kindness and mercy. His kindness prompts Him to declare that we do not have to pay for our waywardness and wrongdoing. The price was already paid by Christ.

This is mind-boggling. God's kindness sets us free from the penalty of our guilt? He has chosen to clear our record instead of punishing us?

Yes.

Even though we might struggle to believe this promise, God's Word is firm: He gives me a clean slate. I do not have to pay the penalty I deserve— He paid it Himself, for me.

Because of His kindness.

 "CANCELED!"

He [God] canceled the record of the charges against us and
took it away by nailing it to the cross.
- COLOSSIANS 2:14 -

Most of us were reluctant. On that Easter morning, we were given a blank slip of paper and asked to write down the things in our lives that we knew did not live up to God's standards. Times that we had been outright disobedient to Him. Attitudes that we knew God wanted to clean out.

To write it all down? Spell out my sins in black and white?

It was a hard thing to do.

The slips were collected, anonymously, and taken to the front, where several men took the papers and began to nail them, one by one, to a wooden cross. The hammering rang out as the service continued. Sometime during that hour, my list of sins went to the cross.

Think about your life: about wrongs you can never make right on your own; acts that weigh heavy on your heart and conscience; dark corners of your mind that still exist in spite of devotion to Christ; and memories of how you have wronged others and purposely rebelled against God's standards.

Think about those things, acknowledge them, and then know that God nailed all those things to Christ's cross and canceled all record of them. Canceled!

Amazing, isn't it?

God says His forgiveness cancels any list of charges against us. Most of us have a pretty long and heavy list.

You remember the apostle Paul, that great missionary devoted to the work of spreading the Gospel? Even he had a terrific struggle with sin. The seventh chapter of Romans gives his account of his constant battle with trying to do the right thing, but failing. He knew the misery we all feel when we find ourselves unable to do and be what we want to do and be. He was, he wrote, "wretched" because the sin living in him was still so strong. What hope was there for him?

The hope was Jesus Christ. Paul wrote with confidence: "So now there is no condemnation for those who belong to Christ Jesus" (Romans 8:1).

No condemnation.

Because Christ paid the price for our misdeeds, God wipes the record clean. For anyone who asks His forgiveness, God tears up the list. Erases everything. Shreds it. Blots out all the black marks.

This is hope, my friend: If you've gone to God

for forgiveness, you can know that those things that have followed you and weighed you down are now gone from God's sight. He refuses to let the record against you stand.

That word *canceled* is a message of freedom.

 **"BELIEVE"**

Everyone who believes in him is declared right with God.
— from ACTS 13:39 —

Those who have lost an arm or a leg often feel the sensation of pain or itching in that limb. The reality is that the leg is gone, but the sense of pain is very real.

In the same way, we may feel we will forever have to carry the burden of guilt for how we have wronged a friend, ruined a relationship, committed terrible sins, and purposely violated God's standards. We are convinced we must somehow pay for our misdeeds. The load of guilt we carry is so heavy that it suffocates any hope that tries to rise.

How can we talk of freedom when we live under this guilt?

Listen to God's reality. God says that Jesus was "beaten so we could be whole. He was whipped so we could be healed" (Isaiah 53:5). He was the one who carried all the punishment for our rebellious ways.

Those things you know you deserve punishment for? The reality is that Jesus has already taken all your guilt and took the punishment Himself.

Isaiah 53 goes on to tell us that because Jesus took our sins on Himself, we are now counted as blameless. We get a clean relationship with God. Jesus bore the guilt—and the penalty—for us (verse 11). And so, "everyone who believes in him is declared right with God" (Acts 13:39).

The world doesn't work this way. But God does. We can trust His kindness and mercy.

We can be certain of this hope concerning our past: Jesus picked up our guilt, paid the penalty for it, and disposed of it. No matter what we might think or feel, God says we are no longer carrying the guilt for what we've done.

 "DECLARES"

For everyone has sinned; we all fall short of God's glorious standard. Yet God, with undeserved kindness, declares that we are righteous. He did this through Christ Jesus when he freed us from the penalty for our sins.

– **ROMANS 3:23-24** –

Did you notice our titles have been focusing on single words? This good news of freedom and forgiveness is so rich and deep that sometimes it helps to focus on specific words that represent the promises. The next amazing word is *declares.*

The news media spotlighted the trial of a man accused of murder. It appeared that everyone knew this man was guilty. Thus, there was shock and outrage when the jury and judge declared him "not guilty." But no matter what everyone thought or felt, no matter whether the accused actually committed murder or not, the verdict came, and the accused was free to go—because the *declaration* was, "not guilty."

God knows how guilty we are. We know we're guilty, and there's no way we can hide anything from God. Yet He declares we are righteous. Other verses say that God declares we are "holy," "cleansed," "blameless," and "without a fault." And we are freed from the penalty for our sins.

Amazing.

I know perfectly well that I am not blameless. I suspect you also will admit to that. We know how far we have strayed from God's standards and how stubborn we have been about choosing our own way and ignoring Him.

But this hope is not dependent on what we can or can't do for ourselves, or on what we have or have not done.

Instead, everything depends on what God says about us—and His kindness says that in spite of anything we've done, if we ask His forgiveness, we are declared *without fault, cleansed, and blameless. Righteous.* He asserts that we are now in good standing with Him. And the price for our waywardness has been paid once and for all.

This is why we can look back at our past—no matter what it holds—and still know hope.

Because His declaration sets us free.

 **"HOME"**

Christ suffered for our sins once for all time. He never sinned,
but he died for sinners to bring you safely home to God.
- from 1 PETER 3:18 -

Why would God offer a pardon for people who spit in His face? Why would Jesus pay such a price to buy our freedom, even though we had no interest in Him? For that matter, why do we have to be freed?

Country music singer Collin Raye performed a song about an eighteen-year-old leaving home, ready to live his own life, and "glad to be gone." Off he goes to a strange and lonely city where, unpacking his things, he finds a note from his mother, a Bible, and a bus ticket home.

God had great and glorious plans for the family He created. Instead, Adam and Eve and all their children decided to choose their own paths. We've twisted and broken all of what God originally pronounced "good." We've ignored God and purposely turned our backs on Him. We've been "glad to be gone."

God's wayward and rebellious creation deserves punishment. But instead, we're offered mercy and forgiveness and an invitation that says, "Come back to Me. Your way has been paid. It's safe to come home."

He still has great and glorious plans for His people. He will free us from everything else so that we can live the lives He created us to have in the first place.

He gave us a ticket back home even while we were still rebelling and running away from Him.

"CONFIDENCE"

So God has given both his promise and his oath... It is impossible for God to lie. Therefore, we who have fled to him for refuge can have great confidence as we hold to the hope that lies before us. This hope is a strong and trustworthy anchor for our souls. It leads us through the curtain into God's inner sanctuary.

– from **HEBREWS 6:18-19** –

We have an enemy, and he thinks he has a powerful weapon against us. Satan works daily to tear holes in our joy, to drain away our trust in God's kindness, and to dim our belief that the record of our past truly has been canceled. His strategy? He slips in and whispers accusations about our past.

But God says we can rebuff those accusations, and we can do it with great confidence!

I don't know where you are as you read this today, but I will tell you where I am—I've fled to God for refuge. I am well aware that in my past, my present, and my future, I'm incapable of living up to God's yardstick. Every day, I fall short. But I'm going forward over a bridge of hope that leads to refuge in His promise of mercy and kindness.

This hope gives us great confidence. It is the anchor that holds us steady. It leads us into the sanctuary of God's presence where there is peace. And it lets us stand there, boldly and with confidence.

We all have regrets. We may be living out the consequences of bad choices. But we can let the past lie in peace and have confidence that, regardless of what we've done, we are now in good standing with God.

He has cleared our record. But what about today and tomorrow? Even though we have this new relationship with God, we still daily fall short of His perfect plan for us. We are still sometimes willful and disobedient.

And God still, daily, forgives His people who ask for His mercy.

Because the penalty we deserve has already been paid.

We'll focus more on this later. For now, know that this hope is certain: The record of our wrongs has been canceled by God's kindness.

That means it's gone!

For more promises that you're free from the penalty,
see the appendix for a list of additional Scriptures.

PRAYER FOR THOSE WHO WALK THE NEW WAY:

Reassure me of your promise.

– from PSALM 119:38 –

FREE TO LIVE
A NEW WAY

 **MY PRISON**

You no longer live under the requirements of the law.
Instead, you live under the freedom of God's grace.
- from **ROMANS 6:14** -

The prison bars that held me were the standards of a "good" life. That might sound strange, but I sat in despair in this prison for many years. Counselors couldn't help me. Self-help books added to the gloom. I would find that only God could rescue me.

From the beginning of time, God has communicated His standards for right living. From the Bible and many other influences, we develop an internal yardstick, a list of dos and don'ts which measure "goodness" or lack thereof.

Do you often despair of ever measuring up? How many times this week have you already missed the mark? Have you lied? Envied? Hated? Uttered an oath? Treated the Sabbath like any other day? Gossiped? Acted selfishly? Attempted revenge?

It's clear we cannot keep ourselves in good standing with God by following a list of dos and don'ts. We'll fall short of the goal, every day. We are guilty, guilty, guilty.

But still I believed that I must make myself acceptable to God by living a "good" life. I was a slave to all the dos and don'ts. It was, truly, a prison.

The problem, of course, was that I could never live up to the standards I read in Scripture. As a matter of fact, I failed in a colossal, awful, destructive way. It took that terrible mess in my life to make me face the fact: I could never be "good enough." No chance of it.

I had made a mess of things, and I deserved any amount of punishment God wanted to order for me.

But, lovingly and gently, He stepped into the middle of the mess and taught me about His grace.

And gave me the gift of hope.

A NEW PLAN FOR UNHOLY DUST

So that we might be made right with God because of our faith in Christ, not because we have obeyed the law. For no one will ever be made right with God by obeying the law.

~ from **GALATIANS 2:16** ~

God knows, the psalmist says, that we are dust. He knows we can never perfectly live out the life that He has said is best.

How could we? His standards are God-sized standards, and we, stubborn and resistant, think we can do things our way instead of His. And off we go, to try exactly that.

In the Old Testament, God chose a people to carry on His work here on the earth, and He made a covenant with them. He promised them blessing, protection, and special privileges, but they were required to do many things in order to maintain a good relationship with God. They were to be God's holy people, and this covenant outlined how they were to live as God's people. It was "the law." And if they broke the covenant in any way, they had specific rituals by which they could gain God's forgiveness.

Yet God's chosen people were just as rebellious and stubborn as we are today; they couldn't live up to the law and keep the covenant. Even rituals of forgiveness could not free them from their sinful bent, cleanse them, or make them perfect and godly. The law only showed how guilty they were, just as my trying to live according to a list of dos and don'ts only made it clear how unable I was to be "good" and "perfect."

Then came Jesus Christ ("at just the right time," Scriptures say!) and the whole story of God's relationship to the world exploded into exciting dimensions.

Everything changed.

Jesus brought a new plan for all of us who are unholy dust.

IT ALL DEPENDS ON JESUS

We are made right with God by placing our faith in Jesus Christ. And this is true for everyone who believes, no matter who we are.
- ROMANS 3:22 -

There's good news from God. He has a plan that sets you and me free from the slavery of worrying about dos and don'ts. This plan says we can be holy before God—and it doesn't depend on us.

Holy? *Me?*

I know my actions and attitudes don't deserve the label "holy." You'll probably admit that about yourself, too. At the turning point of my life, I was forced to admit that nothing I could do would ever bring me to *holy.* Not even close. I daily fail to live up to God's standards.

God's plan is that Christ has paid the price for all of our messes, our rebellion, and our transgressions. *All people* can be forgiven their breaking of God's laws and can enjoy a good standing before God.

Our standing with God is now based solely on what Jesus did. It's not dependent on what we do or don't do, or on what we are or what we are not. It all depends on what Jesus did for us, when He took the punishment for us. And what He did is good for everyone who believes, for all time (see Hebrews 10:10).

To put it in the human realm of experience— have you ever had someone "go to bat" or "put in a good word" for you? And then you moved ahead, trusting that what this person has done for you has paved your way forward?

Christ is the one Mediator who can reconcile

God and humanity—God and *me* (1 Timothy 2:5). What Christ did has paved the way for me to be able to stand before God with a clean record. I'm going forward, depending on that certainty.

If we put our faith in what this Mediator has done for us, then we are even considered "holy" in His sight.

Being holy does not mean we are perfect.

It does mean we have a new relationship to God, He has a purpose for us, we are free of the slavery to our old nature, and God is changing us. (We'll talk about all those later.)

If we believe in what Jesus did for us, we have a new status before God. It all depends on what Jesus did, not on what I can or can't do.

I can't depend on myself to make myself "good enough." It's impossible. Jesus announced there's a new way. We don't deserve it, but God offers it to us anyway.

 BREAKING LIGHT OF MORNING

Because of God's tender mercy, the morning light from
heaven is about to break upon us, to give light to those who
sit in darkness and in the shadow of death, and to guide us
to the path of peace.

– LUKE 1:78-79 –

It was scandalous, really. Great waves of con-
sternation swept through the religious establish-
ment as Jesus, the teacher from Nazareth, began
to be popular with the crowds.

The man kept company with the wrong people, for one thing. He did things on the Sabbath
that were forbidden. And the things He was saying! He would preface His teaching with, "The old
law said thus and such, but God is offering you
a new, better way to live and think." He claimed
to be introducing God's new covenant. Imagine!
Bucking the old, traditional system. Inciting people to abandon the old laws!

Jesus' message was that there was a new
way coming.

In the old covenant, God said, "Obey me, and
I'll forgive your sins and bless you in every way.
If you don't obey, you will be punished." The new
covenant says, "Your transgressions are forgiven
because Jesus took your punishment. Believe and
trust this, and you will inherit everything I've
promised my people."

Does that mean God no longer gives us standards for living? Of course not! (Romans 6:1-2) He still lays out His guidelines for His children, but His forgiveness brings freedom from the guilt of falling short. Freedom from slavery to dos and don'ts. Freedom from worry that I'm not "good enough."

Living by a checklist, we always have that record standing between us and our Creator. Our record, with big black marks against us, raises a barrier between us and God, who wants to bring us back to Himself. We can never be "good enough."

Instead, God made a new way for us to be right with Him.

He offers us *mercy*—an undeserved forgiveness. And that mercy breaks the barrier between us. We can come to Him freely. The burden of "performance" is rolled away, and we can enter into a new relationship with our Creator. We're now living, not under a dark, heavy, guilty record, but under the freedom that this mercy has granted us (Romans 6:14).

The words of the opening Scripture were spoken by Zechariah, a priest who was given a glimpse of what this new way of living looked like. He compared Jesus' coming to earth to the coming of morning light. Jesus was bringing a new day of freedom and peace.

And hope.

All given to us from the hand of God's mercy.

~~ SO THAT HE COULD ADOPT US ~~

God sent [Jesus] to buy freedom for us who were slaves to
the law, so that he could adopt us as his very own children.
- GALATIANS 4:5 -

God's mercy and forgiveness dissolve the
barrier between us and Him, and He says we can
freely come back to Him.

Think about our history with Him. He created the human race, but we said, "We're going
to do things our own way. We want nothing to
do with you."

In other words, God's creation set itself up as
His enemy.

It wasn't just Adam and Eve. Every one of us
has done that on a personal level, too.

At our human level, such a rebellion and rejec-
tion would set the stage for ongoing hostilities and
retaliation—all-out war. God could have wiped us
out in His wrath. We are, after all, just a breath.
His curse could have pronounced a sentence of
misery and death with no hope of pardon.

Yet, Scripture says, God's offer of forgiveness reaches out to His enemies. Mercy is not

deserved, but He makes the offer anyway; that's *grace*.

The law God laid down would have condemned us all. But He offers us freedom from condemnation, and instead of living as enemies of our Creator, we will be adopted as sons and daughters of the Almighty Lord of the universe. We become part of the family of God.

That's an amazing thing.

Hope hears this message: God is willing to wipe my transgressions off the record and give me His name. He will call me His own.

UNDESERVED PRIVILEGE

Because of our faith, Christ has brought us into this place
of undeserved privilege where we now stand, and we
confidently and joyfully look forward to sharing God's glory.

- ROMANS 5:2 -

I was traveling, and one morning at the breakfast buffet in the hotel, I heard a short exchange.

"Good morning," greeted one person. "How are you this morning?"

The man replied, "I'm so good. God is so much better to me than I deserve."

Ah, I thought. *That sums up exactly this*

whole life of hope we live. Our hope is founded on this: God is so much better to us than we could *ever* deserve.

Jesus said He came to give life, rich and satisfying life (John 10:10). For those who have known that verse for years and years, the words easily roll off the tongue. But what does it mean? What is life, rich and satisfying?

The apostle Paul sums it up pretty well in the first verses of Romans 5. Take a minute to go back and read the opening verse.

Look at those promises: Undeserved privilege. Joy. Confidence. A share in God's glory. And the following verse (which I didn't include here) says that even when we do run into problems, we will still have reason to rejoice.

In these days, who can claim such a life?

Everyone who is adopted by God is given this hope!

And there is that word *hope* again. What hope is there in this world? Only the hope held in the promises God makes to His people. This hope, when it takes root in us, will grow joy and peace and confidence.

And undeserved privileges. That intrigues me. Doesn't that interest you? What are those privileges? We look at those privileges in detail in another Hope Knows book, *Getting Through Today.*

Jesus can take us from guilt and condemnation to undeserved privilege. He's given us a new way to live fully and richly.

BE BOLD, FULLY TRUSTING

And so, dear brothers and sisters, we can boldly enter heaven's Most Holy Place because of the blood of Jesus. Let us go right into the presence of God with sincere hearts fully trusting him.

- from **HEBREWS 10:19, 22** -

Hope knows the old yardstick is gone; a new way of faith has come (Galatians 3). This certainty frees us: No matter who we are or what we've done, we are right with God if we accept the gift of Jesus' atonement for our sins.

Did you notice the exciting words that jump out of the verses above? *Boldly. Right into His presence. Fully trusting Him.*

No need to doubt or waver. As those who have been named sons and daughters of God, we can go right into His presence, boldly, with a clean conscience, opening our hearts to Him. We no longer have a curtain of sin keeping us from the holy presence of the Lord. Christ's death ripped that barrier apart. And we can trust that Jesus is still standing before God, representing us.

We have a new way to know God and a new way to think about our lives here on earth. Jesus opened that way for us.

We can be sure of it; we can trust God to keep all His promises about our past, our relationship to Him, and the new way He is offering us.

And we can walk that way boldly.

To soak up more hope of being free to live in a new way, see the appendix for a list of additional Scriptures.

**PRAYER WHEN BATTLING
THE OLD SELF:**

O Lord, you alone are my hope.

– from PSALM 71:5 –

FREE FROM MY OLD SELF

 RESCUE FROM MYSELF

Therefore, dear brothers and sisters, you have no obligation
to do what your sinful nature urges you to do.

– ROMANS 8:12 –

Rescue and freedom for us. This is good news.
But can Jesus rescue me from *me?*

It's easy to sit in church and look and sound
like a Christian. But how do I sound when I walk
out of church and see someone slam their car door
against my beautiful new car? What happens

inside me when I hear gossip spread by an old enemy? When scars from old hurts still ache, how can I ever forgive the person who caused those scars?

Old habits and deeply ingrained sins have put down stubborn roots in our lives. The devil whispers lies: "You can't change this." "How can this thing between you and your husband ever be healed?" "It's impossible to forgive her." "You are only human, after all..."

What we call "human nature" is constantly trying to push us down paths contrary to how Christ taught us to live.

"I can't help it. That's just the way I am." That's an excuse we often use.

Scriptures tell us that we will always have that selfish and rebellious nature within us, and that old nature fights against all our good intentions and our desire to obey God.

But hope hears and believes and lives by the promises of God, and He has made this spectacular declaration: The control that selfishness and sin once had on our lives is ended. Over. Done with.

Take a moment to read (again) the opening Scripture. I didn't want you to miss it—because, to my mind, this is one of the most amazing, freeing, and hope-full promises that God makes to His people.

I always have to smile (guiltily) when I read that verse in Romans 8:12. That word *obligation* brushes aside all our excuses, doesn't it? We sometimes feel we have an excuse, a compulsion, some irresistible force that makes us follow our human nature. After all, we reason, it's "logical" or "understandable" that we feel and react in certain ways, isn't it?

God says, "Nope. You never have to give in to human nature again. It is no longer your master."

To my mind, that is an amazing, wonderful, welcome promise.

HEALED BY WOUNDS

He [Christ] personally carried our sins in his body on the cross so that we can be dead to sin and live for what is right. By his wounds you are healed.

— 1 PETER 2:24 —

Can we really live out that promise that we don't have to follow our human nature?

We've all experienced the same frustration: Our good intentions, our will, and our determination to change are all too often overwhelmed and overthrown by old attitudes and habits.

Most likely, we've all had similar experiences.

We try to change ourselves. We desperately want to change. But we've been defeated so many times. Created to be like God, our humanness now suffers from the sickness of sin. When we want to be something different or we want to do something different—something good and holy—those tendencies we call human nature (now corrupted) always seem to get in the way.

How do we shake ourselves free of the old so that we can move on to the holy intentions we want to pursue? To live the kind of lives God always meant for us to live?

How can we do away with the old and make ourselves new?

We don't.

We can't.

And we know we can't.

The apostle Paul had the same struggle. He asked the same questions. And then he wrote, "Thank God! The answer is in Jesus Christ our Lord" (Romans 7:25).

God says that Christ not only paid the penalty for what I've done, but the beatings, injuries, and agony He endured made it possible for me to be free of the power of my old, corrupted nature.

I can't explain or understand how this happens, but God says this is reality. This is one of the results of that dark day when Jesus hung on a cross.

Jesus didn't come to condemn the world, wrote Jesus' very close friend (John 3:17), but to save the world—to save us from everything that keeps us from enjoying the life God intended us to have in the first place. That includes healing the diseases that plague us.

Why not live in God's reality? Imagine being free of the power of all that old "stuff" that has controlled you for too long! I want that. I want to live in that reality.

This is the promise that hope knows and lives: Somehow, what Jesus submitted to on the cross now makes it possible for my own brokenness to be healed. I'm no longer a slave to the old me; I am free to live a new life.

Thank God!

DEATH AT THE CROSSROADS

We know that our old sinful selves were crucified with Christ so that sin might lose its power in our lives. We are no longer slaves to sin. For when we died with Christ we were set free from the power of sin. When he died, he died once to break the power of sin.

- from **ROMANS 6:6-7, 10** -

To be free of our old selves, we must be willing to die.

When we make the choice to become followers of Christ, He says we must do exactly that—follow Him. We must follow, not only in actions and attitudes, but we must also follow His example and die.

What's that about?

The apostle Paul writes of nailing our own selfish ambitions and passions to Christ's cross; we are "crucified with Christ."

What does this "dying" mean? It means we consent to letting go of our old life, our old habits, our old attitudes and ways of thinking and acting. We make the choice to give up "our way" and begin to follow Christ and His way.

Jesus says that unless we "die" to the old, we cannot take hold of the new life God has for us.

If I want to live in Montana, I must let go of my life in Ohio. Makes sense, doesn't it? To move to a new life, we must leave another life behind. You cannot live in both the kingdom of darkness and the kingdom of light. If I did actually move to Montana, many things would often still call me back to Ohio. That same thing happens when I move to the kingdom of light; many things try to call me back to the kingdom of darkness. (We'll look at how Jesus helps us with that.)

The point is, there is a decision to be made. At this crossroads, we must make the choice:

Will we "die with Christ" and let the One who came to rescue us break the power of the old self within us?

He can free us from that old life. We cannot free ourselves, but He has the power and He said He would do it. It's the only way to be free from what we call our human nature. It's the only way to be free from the tyranny of our self-centeredness, our moods, our anger, our impatience, our lack of love, and our unfaithfulness. Christ has already suffered the consequences of all the darkness within us; we do not need to be prisoners of that old self.

But we must consent to let the old die. If we make that decision, then the power of what Christ did on the cross somehow takes effect in us, and God declares our slavery to our human nature is over. He honors our desire for a new life and keeps His promise that we'll be set free from the old.

It seems beyond possible, doesn't it?

But God says it *is* possible.

The choice is ours. The power to free and heal is Christ's.

RESURRECTION (OURS)

For we died and were buried with Christ by baptism. And just as Christ was raised from the dead by the glorious power of the Father, now we also may live new lives.
- ROMANS 6:4 -

Christ came to do for us everything we could not do ourselves. And amazing things happened on the cross and in the grave where Jesus was buried.

We can't explain it all, but God tells us we can be sure of these things:

- Jesus' death freed us from that old, old problem of guilt before God. We are no longer living under His condemnation.

- And then, Jesus came back from death, broke its power, and is alive today.

- That same power that gave Jesus new life will bring new life to us, too.

As we now talk about resurrection, I'm not jumping ahead, looking into the future toward the day we too are raised from physical death to the next life. That will also happen. But our hope knows that we have already experienced a death and resurrection. The "old" in us has died. We have been given a new life.

By the glorious power of the Father. That's where our hope lies. We can't explain it or define it or describe it. It's a supernatural power beyond anything we can imagine. Yes, we are talking about power beyond what we know as the "natural" world. It's a power that can bring someone out of death. That's a power that can certainly give us new lives, too!

And this is one reason why hope lives in great expectation—we've been given a glimpse of God's all-encompassing, ultimate plan: He's still creating, still doing new things, still bringing new life out of death. His objective is not simply to condemn this rebellious world. He wants to make all things new. And Christ came to lead the way and to tell us it can be done.

The power of the old life is broken. His power brings new life.

We'll think more about this new life in a few pages, but for now, celebrate that the power of the old is broken!

Now we also may live resurrected lives, every day.

 THE MIGHTY POWER AT WORK

And with [Christ] you were raised to new life because you
trusted the mighty power of God, who raised
Christ from the dead.

- from **COLOSSIANS 2:12** -

Here's more good news: God does not say we have to produce a new life on our own power. Isn't that a relief?

For a long time, I thought this "dying" only meant that I should, by my own sheer willpower, put all my old attitudes and behavior behind me. Get rid of that old, sinful stuff! Be more like Christ! Create a new me!

That didn't work out so well. (My willpower going against my old nature? Willpower doesn't stand a chance. I don't have the strength to give myself this new life.)

But the power of the Spirit of God? Now there's something that can do amazing things.

I guess each person will have to stop right here and answer a question: Do you believe in the power of an Almighty God?

Maybe you have seen so much of "human nature" that you just can't believe that people can change their character... but do you believe *God* can change a person's character?

God says that "the power of the life-giving

Spirit" will free those who belong to Christ from the power of their sinful nature. No longer does that nature control us (Romans 8:2, 9).

And that's the key—our hope trusts His power, not ours. Our hope focuses on what He can do, not on what we can do.

Our lives are battlegrounds. Scriptures don't sugar-coat the reality of our situation: As long as we live on this earth, our old human nature will want the opposite of what Christ wants to do in our new life.

So what is our hope?

Our hope is that Christ's power is greater than all the old habits, thinking, and emotions that held us captive. The old nature dies, bit by bit, as God's power works in us to defeat the old powers that controlled us.

We can trust God to do what He says He will do. And as we move away from the old, we look forward to the unfolding of the new.

This is His plan—to set us free from the prison of the old self and to make every part of our lives new.

For more promises of freedom from your old self,
see the appendix for a list of additional Scriptures.

**PRAYER FOR MOVING
INTO NEW LIFE:**

*Open my eyes to see the wonderful
truths in your instructions.*

— **PSALM 119:18** —

NEW LIFE

 MAKING ALL THINGS NEW

Anyone who belongs to Christ has become a new person.
The old life is gone; a new life has begun!

- **2 CORINTHIANS 5:17** -

Death and resurrection. That's one way the Scriptures describe what God promises us when we believe in Christ. Another way the change in us is explained is as a new birth.

Birth. Think of all the things that word implies. A brand new life coming into existence. The creation and beginning of something completely new.

Haven't we all longed for that at some time?

God says that's what He does for those who believe in Christ—He begins a new life! He creates something completely new.

The old is gone. Its power is broken. Your new life is here, birthed, begun, and nourished by the Spirit of God, as God creates a new you.

That's breathtaking.

This is our hope, what God promises and we can expect in our lives: His creation is not yet finished. He is still creating and still doing new things—things we have not imagined and cannot imagine.

In every one of His children's lives, God is doing something new. We are part of His new creation that prophecy foresaw!

We'll be thinking about all these new things God has for us, but we will need some help to see things in a *new* way.

That's why, in preparation, we have used Psalm 119:18 as the prayer for this section. We'll ask for new eyes to see God's truth.

So as we begin to think about the hope of new life, we pray,

Spirit, open our eyes to see these wonderful truths, the bridges of hope that are strong beneath us and keep us moving onward with confidence and expectation.

FOR THOSE WHO BELONG TO CHRIST

But to all who believed [Christ] and accepted him, he gave
the right to become children of God. They are reborn - not
with a physical birth resulting from human passion or plan,
but a birth that comes from God.

- JOHN 1:12-13 -

"If I could live my life over again..."

How many people have said those words! Maybe the wish has come from your own lips. Most of us wouldn't want to go back to our actual birth and early childhood, but if only we could go back and be given a second chance at some parts of our life history!

But let's be honest—do you think that second go-round would be much different than the first? We all know how prone we are to repeating our mistakes and falling into the same behavior, over and over again. What we need is not a "do-over." What we need is to be a completely new person. A new life. New beginnings.

Scripture tells us this is possible.

The Scripture says we are reborn. A birth that comes from God marks a new beginning, the new life we long for, because this birth brings alive in us the life God created men and women to have in the first place.

It is a new life, with a new connection to the God of all hope.

And it all begins with believing Christ. "Anyone who believes in God's Son has eternal life," wrote John (John 3:36).

This *eternal life* is not only a never-ending life, as we normally define *eternal life,* but it is also a brand new kind of life in quality, in the way it is lived, and in its privileges and benefits. It is, in short, a life on a *heavenly* plane. God is offering to His children, right now, the benefits of such a life. We'll think more about that in a few pages.

But first, what are the requirements set out for receiving this new life? Who can have it?

Scripture does not say—

Anyone who can overcome their bad habits, or *Anyone whose behavior meets God's standards,* or *Anyone who has enough faith.*

No, it does not even say, *Anyone who wants to change their life badly enough.*

Instead, God's promise is this: Anyone who belongs to Christ is a new person and has an eternal, heavenly life.

So, if that's you, if you believe in and belong to Christ, then let's think about your new life.

And about the old life being gone.

And the new that is now here.

～ THE CERTAINTY ～

*When God our Savior revealed his kindness and love, he
saved us, not because of the righteous things we had done,
but because of his mercy. He washed away our sins, giving
us a new birth and new life through the Holy Spirit.*

– TITUS 3:4,5 –

A new life? Can we believe that?

What if our birth into this new life has not been
accompanied by immediate, dramatic changes in
our circumstances, nature, or feelings? Here we
are, in the same situations we have always lived
in. Faced with the same struggles. A new life, you
say? Where? How? When?

A highly educated religious teacher sat
face-to-face with Jesus and voiced some of the
same questions. Even then, he had difficulty
understanding what Jesus was telling him. He
wanted the "how" of everything explained, but
Jesus said the new life that the Holy Spirit brings
to believers is much like the wind. It cannot be
defined, detailed, measured, explained—but you
can see the effects. (John 3)

God says He birthed a new life in you, a life
that comes from His Spirit. It's the beginning of
something brand new.

The new life that is given to those who believe
is nothing like our earthly life measured in years,
marked with a beginning and an end, limited by

our earthly capabilities and natures. This new life is given by God, and it's God-designed and God-sized. It's unlimited, built upon the Almighty's capabilities and His nature. The Scriptures say we were originally created in God's image, to be like Him (Genesis 1:26). Amazing. God is still creating in His image, and He has big plans for His children.

The question before you now is this: Do you believe this promise? That is the requirement for the old to be gone and the new to come.

At times, we all struggle with doubt and flagging belief. I know of only one answer to such times: the prayer, *Help my unbelief!* The heavenly Father always hears and answers those honest prayers.

As we go forward, we'll hear our Father's Word on some of our questions, but this new life is not something we'll ever be able to explain with logic or science or even theology.

Our faith simply stands on the bridge of hope and says, "I believe this because God says it is so. I am trusting in this reality."

God's Word assures us of these truths: He has freed us and provided a way to come back to Him. He has adopted us and named us His children. Now He is making our lives—in other words, every bit of us—completely new. We are part of His new creation!

This is His promise, the bridge laid down before us. Our faith crosses this bridge to go toward everything He has for us.

A new life: It really is possible.

THE NEW CREATION HAS COME

And just as Christ was raised from the dead by the glorious power of the Father, now we also may live new lives.
– from **ROMANS 6:4** –

Here it is, in a nutshell: When we came to Christ, we buried the old life. And then God gave us new lives. We became part of Christ's new creation.

Just as Christ left his earthly life behind and lives in a resurrected body, we leave behind our old lives and live in a new dimension of life.

Instead of becoming a new person by my own self-discipline and will (which never worked out well), what is happening now is that God is creating me anew. He is shaping me into a new person.

Or, to put myself in the big picture of God's plan to make all things new, I have become part of His new creation! The life He gave me belongs to the new creation world, not to this old, sin-corrupted, decaying, dying one.

Christ's resurrection began that process of new creation. In the book of John's Revelation, Christ refers to Himself as "the beginning of God's new creation" (Revelation 3:14).

In my Bible, the word *beginning* is asterisked, and the footnote expands on the word, stating that it could also be translated as *the ruler* or *the source.*

Christ is the source, the beginning, the ruler of God's new creation. In Paul's letter to the Corinthians, he calls Christ the "firstfruit" of those God raised from the dead. He is the first to be resurrected to new life, and many other sons and daughters will follow.

That resurrection of sons and daughters is not referring only to resurrection after physical death, on some future day. That will come eventually. But we are also resurrected, born to a new kind of life, today, here, now. We have a new connection to God (and to others in the Kingdom), He gives us a new heart, we have a new power for living, a new purpose and mission on earth—all things we're going to take a look at in the next pages.

We close the book on the old, and God begins His new creation within us.

 INTO HEAVENLY REALMS

For he raised us from the dead along with Christ and seated us with him in the heavenly realms because we are united with Christ Jesus.

- **EPHESIANS 2:6** -

What does this new, resurrected, re-birthed life look like?

At first glance, or to casual observers, it might look very much like those old lives that the Scriptures say are gone. We live in the same circumstances. The same internal battles still rage. We are still here, still in the same world, still with the same body. But take a look at the verse above.

What? We're seated in the heavenly realms? What could that mean?

It's a metaphor, something much like our sayings of "She has a place at the table," or "He's climbed pretty far up the ladder."

You've been brought into the realms of heaven itself. Come in. Have a seat, right here, with our Lord Jesus. You are a part of this now, you belong to this realm now. Your life is no longer confined to earthly limits; you are now living in heavenly dimensions.

We catch a glimpse of this when we read Jesus' words that those who listen to His message and believe in God "have eternal life. They will never be condemned for their sins, but they have already passed from death into life" (John 5:24).

For many of us, the phrase that leaps out is the assurance that we will not be condemned. We so desperately need mercy, and those words are what we hear. But think about the last sentence: "They have already passed from death to life."

Now, we all know we are dying. It is the one thing on earth we all have in common, something ahead of us that we know must be a part of this earthly life. But Jesus has said that those who believe have already—right now!—passed from death to life.

This can only mean that we are now living on another plane. We have been given a life that is more than this physical body and its limitations. It's a life that does not know death. We are still on a pilgrimage through earthly years, but we have been born into a life that will not end in oblivion.

And this new life is in heavenly realms.

We truly are breathing new air.

This is a statement of who and where we are today—Christ has brought us into God's kingdom right now. We are His people. As His children, we have heavenly privileges and blessings now, even while we still live in this time and space—that's the new, eternal life we've been given.

In the first chapter of Ephesians, Paul wrote that we've been blessed with all the spiritual blessings of the heavenly realms because we belong to Christ Jesus. We might be living on this earth, still walking through its battles, still fighting the corruption of our humanity, still faced with physical decaying and dying—but we have been given a life that goes beyond those limits and is blessed with all the resources of heaven. This hope we have of a "heavenly" life is not limited to a life after death, someday, somewhere. It is a life already begun, and it now is in God's dimensions of life.

We set our sights on new realities—the realities of God's sphere, His Kingdom, His heaven, His mission, and His plans. God shares with us heavenly resources that go beyond the limits of earthly life. Yes! Everything is truly new.

Here again, our human minds will never fully understand this; only faith in what God says enables us to catch glimpses of this fantastic truth. (Remember the Psalm prayer for this section.)

I think God gives us those glimpses to encourage us. On this side of heaven, we'll never be able to take it all in or plumb the depths of this reality, but the Spirit will give us glimpses of the limitless life we've inherited.

And with each glimpse, He tells us, *"This* is your life now, my child."

 BUT THE OLD ISN'T GONE, IS IT?

My old self has been crucified with Christ. It is no longer
I who live, but Christ lives in me. So I live in this earthly
body by trusting in the Son of God, who loved
me and gave himself for me.

- GALATIANS 2:20 -

I may be tempted to observe (complain?) that very much of my "old" life is still very much right here, right now.

What do you suppose the Scripture means when it says that the old is "gone"?

I know my old nature is not dead. It still fights the Spirit within me, every day. The Scripture says this will be reality as long as we're in this world.

But my old nature no longer rules!

As a matter of fact, nothing from the old life holds ultimate power anymore. Yes, old attitudes still try to steer me down wrong paths. Yes, some circumstances of my life are still trying. Yes, this body is headed back toward the dust.

But the old is dead because its power is defeated. Its strength is broken. Its reign in my life is over. As a frivolous example, have you ever said, "Donuts are dead to me?" Donuts haven't disappeared from your life; but they've lost their power.

So it is with the old nature that used to rule you.

When we become part of the heavenly realm, new things come, and the new can and will push out and displace the old. The old life no longer rules. It tries to fight back, but Life pushes out Death. The Holy Spirit defeats the old nature. Freedom breaks chains. God's new creation foils Satan's destructive plans. Eternity trumps the earthly.

In the opening Scripture, the apostle Paul acknowledges that he is still living in an earthly body—and having to deal with all of what we call "human nature," the *old* in us. Even the great apostle Paul still had old desires and attitudes rise up and try to lure him into taking a wrong path.

So, how do we live with this situation?

By trusting Jesus. We will see, as we go on, how Jesus supplies what we need while we are living as earthly beings who have a heavenly life. This provision for us is a huge part of our hope; we depend on it.

We all have certain Scriptures that are like shining lights for us. They show us possibilities, beckoning us forward and standing out there ahead of us, saying, *Come, see what wonderful things are waiting for you.*

One of those beacons for me is a phrase from

2 Corinthians 5:4. The context of the verse is a letter Paul wrote about the new bodies God has promised us after physical death, and he says, "these dying bodies will be swallowed up by life." In an earlier letter, he also wrote about "mortal bodies transformed into immortal bodies" (1 Corinthians 15:53).

I've come to think of these phrases as applying to all of me, not just my body.

I want all of the mortal to be swallowed up by the immortal.

All of the old to be swallowed up by the new.

All of the dying to be swallowed up by Life.

All the imperfect to be made perfect.

All of the earthly to be swallowed up by the heavenly.

And that's what our Heavenly Father has promised He is doing for His children.

It's happening right now for those who believe and hold this hope.

For more assurance that you have a new life,
see the appendix for a list of additional Scriptures.

PRAYER OF THANKS:

[Lord,] you have endowed [me] with eternal blessings and given [me] the joy of your presence.

– **ADAPTED from PSALM 21:6** –

NEW ACCESS
TO GOD

"COME, AND DON'T BE AFRAID"

Christ's one act of righteousness brings a right relationship
with God and new life for everyone.
– from ROMANS 5:18 –

They were seasoned fisherman, but at that
moment, they were worried—and scared, too.

Their nets came up heavy, filled with
shining, squirming fish. But their joy at the
amazing catch was short-lived. The web of nets
was beginning to tear, and the boat, rocking

violently, was sinking lower and lower under its load. The fishermen shouted back to shore for another boat and more help.

In the middle of all the commotion, they were stunned to see their boss, Simon, fall to his knees in front of the man who had come out fishing with them.

The man had shown up just as they were stowing their gear after a long, unsuccessful night on the lake.

"Go out where the water's deeper and throw in your nets. Let's get those fish!" he had told Simon.

Simon was probably thinking of the many times they'd come up empty all night long, of the repeated disappointment, and of the weariness aching in his bones. Fishing was just not good that day. He began to explain, "We worked all night and didn't catch a thing."

But something made him stop his objections and obey. Did he hear a certain tone of authority? Did he catch a certain look in the man's eye? Whatever made him change his mind, Simon gave in. "But if you say so..." Then he had given the orders to go out again. And the man got in the boat and went with them.

Now, in the midst of the excited activity and frantic calling for more help, Simon looked at Jesus, sitting there in his boat. (I have a feeling Jesus was smiling.) This catch was a miracle, and Simon knew this man was responsible. Whoever this Jesus was, surely he was a powerful man of God.

Simon fell to his knees in front of him—and uttered what we might think a very strange thing: "Please go away from me! I'm too much of a sinner to be in your presence!"

Simon knew his unworthiness. He came from a long tradition of worship that said in order to approach God, you had to offer the right sacrifices, in the right way, and through a proper priest. Ceremonial cleansing was a detailed matter and everything was outlined for the Jews—the correct procedures, times, places, and even the clothing the priest wore to offer the sacrifice. In the Temples of the Old Testament, those who didn't follow the rules could be struck dead for daring to approach the holiness of God in the wrong way.

Yes, Simon was afraid. He knew he was not fit to be anywhere near this holy man. But Jesus replied:

"Don't be afraid. Come, Simon, join up with me, and you'll be fishing for people."

He was inviting Simon into a new relationship with Him.

Simon did go with Jesus, and he watched in the coming months as Jesus extended the astonishing invitation to all sorts of people—people who knew very well they were unfit to be in the presence of a holy and almighty God. The message must have been puzzling to those who had grown up under layer upon layer of rules about how to approach God. On the one hand, this man was claiming to be the Son of God, yet He said, simply, "Come. And don't be afraid."

They went to parties with tax collectors—scumbags and scoundrels, every one of them. Liars. Cheaters. Thieves. Adulterers. And when Jesus was criticized for his choice of social company, He shot back, "This is why I'm here—I'm looking for those who know they are sinners and need to repent" (from Luke 5:31).

It was a new ball game. The old way of thinking was that you had to be cleansed and worthy to approach God. But who of us is ever that clean? Jesus, though, opened the door to everyone who knows they are not deserving or worthy.

His message was and still is that God has swung open His door and now says, "Come. And don't be afraid."

 WITHOUT A SINGLE FAULT?

Now all glory to God, who is able to keep you from falling
away and will bring you with great joy into his glorious
presence without a single fault.

– JUDE 1:24 –

When you think of Almighty God, where are you in the picture?

Do you slink away from His presence, hoping He's too busy with others to notice you and your life? Are you cringing before Him, thinking of your unworthiness and that He must surely be disappointed in you? Or are you standing before Him, confident, free, and without a single fault, basking in His glorious presence? Maybe even dancing in freedom and joy?

We might be very much like Simon. We know the condition of our hearts and minds. And maybe we have this feeling that if we do come into God's presence, He will be frowning and pronouncing judgment.

But what does hope, living on the promises of God, tell us?

Jude, the half-brother of Jesus, wrote the words of our opening Scripture, a beautiful benediction for the lives of believers.

How is it possible to come to God without a single fault?

I know the faults of my own life; I know I am not blameless. I acknowledge blots on my soul that would separate me from a holy and just God. How can I come into His presence with a clean slate and clear conscience?

I know who and what I have been. How can I possibly hope that the picture of standing *blameless* in God's presence could ever be a picture *of me?*

Christ is the Rescuer. The One who came to do everything for us that we cannot do ourselves. And that includes being able to come into the presence of a holy, holy God, and stand there, without a single fault.

Picture yourself there. See yourself in the Father's presence, instead of a rebellious child awaiting punishment, now a much-loved son or daughter being given great privileges.

And don't forget to add great joy to the picture!

Once you have that picture firmly in mind, let's go on to see how it *is* possible.

 THE BARRIER TORN APART

By his death, Jesus opened a new and life-giving way
through the curtain into the Most Holy Place.

– **HEBREWS 10:20** –

Imagine you are a priest in the Temple of Jesus' time. You are there because you were born into a privileged family of priests, the lineage that carried special responsibilities in the Temple.

Yet even you cannot venture behind the heavy curtain hanging in the Temple, shutting off the room called the Holy of Holies. Behind that curtain is the Ark of the Covenant, the place of God's presence here in the Temple. Only the high priest can approach God in that sacred place, and he enters only one time a year, after he has completed a regimen of purification and preparation that makes him acceptable to stand in the presence of the Almighty. Any other person who enters at any other time and in any other way will be struck dead. You have known this all your life. You are in awe of the presence of Almighty God, but you, even in your special position as priest, are very, very careful to observe all the laws, every detail, about the proper way to approach God.

On this afternoon, you go about your duties but your thoughts are not in the Temple. The grapevine is sizzling with the news: that man who called himself the Son of God, who has stirred up your people with outlandish teaching and sensational miracles, is being executed. He was arrested last night. Your mind goes to that place outside the city where criminals are put to death for their crimes. Finally, you think, there will be an end to the turmoil of the last three years.

Suddenly you feel dizzy. Then you realize the earth itself is moving. The floor of the Temple is shifting under your feet. You lose your balance and fall to your knees as shouts tell of the terrified confusion of other priests.

The heavy curtain, thicker than a man's hand, is tearing from the top to the bottom. Sixty feet in the air, the elaborately embroidered cloth is beginning to rip apart, as though an unseen hand is tearing away the barrier between you and the Holy of Holies. Admittance into the presence of the holy God is laid open to anyone and everyone.

You will hear more news later, as the city buzzes about the afternoon's events. And as you and your friends piece together the information you hear, you will realize that the tearing apart of the curtain came at the very moment that that man, Jesus, died.

That account is probably my favorite story in the entire Bible. Come to think of it, it is actually *the* story of the entire Bible. The Gospel writers tell it in just one short, dramatic line.

Imagine the thick curtain beginning to split at the very top, the tear slowly moving downward. Hear the ripping of fabric. Watch the richly colored threads falling apart as the way opens up into the Most Holy Place of God's presence, the place where very few ever dared to enter.

God was making a dramatic statement. A barrier had hung between God and mankind for centuries. Now He was telling the world that He was changing His relationship to all of humanity.

Jesus died, and the barrier between God and humanity was torn apart.

Jesus' death did away with all the barriers between us and God. His blood blotted out the sin in our lives that separated us from God. He died so men and women could once again have a relationship with their Creator, a relationship as free and intimate as Adam and Eve once had with God.

Paul wrote in Colossians that we were enemies of God, but He opened the way of reconciliation through the death of Christ, and "as a result, he has brought you into his own presence, and you are holy and blameless as you stand before him without a single fault" (Colossians 1:22).

There is that phrase again: "without a single fault." Somehow, the blood that flowed from the body of Christ wiped away my guilt. Every bit of it!

And now He has ushered me into His presence, and I stand blameless before Him. I can come freely, without guilt or fear.

How that can be possible is beyond my comprehension. It's a mystery.

But it is the absolute, certain hope that changed my life.

 **LOVE PURSUING YOU**

Even before he made the world, God loved us.
- from EPHESIANS 1:4 -

Aren't those nine words above amazing?

Consider the timeline. Well, we hardly know how to consider it, because our measurement of time doesn't give us a way to handle "before the world began."

But this one line that God inspired Paul to write tells us that before He made the world, He loved us.

Before He made the world? Before time began?

I don't understand this, I cannot grasp it, but I choose to believe that what God says of Himself is true. Before time began, He loved the people He created. Amazing.

God created men and women to live on—and enjoy—the earth and to live in friendship with Him. Instead, they chose to turn their backs on Him and live with no regard for their Creator.

We don't often think of God as having emotions like sorrow and regret, but I think God uses our human language of emotions so that we can begin to understand Him. And so we find it there in Scripture: When humanity turned away from God, it broke His heart (Genesis 6:6).

And that "broken heart" phrase does not sound exaggerated when we see what God did to bring people back into a friendship with Him. He took extreme measures. He came into our history as one of us to die for us, to repair our friendship with Him, even "while we were still sinners" (Romans 5:8-9). Before we even cared whether or not we knew God, He had made a way for us to come back to Him.

He decided to come into our dark and corrupted world, and live and suffer and die as a human being who experienced all the pain and joy we experience. God chose to do that. And it was all to offer us a friendship with Him.

Today, ponder the love that pursues you. Love that existed before the world was in place. Love with a heart that breaks when we turn our backs and go our own way. Love that is willing to come into our dark world and suffer with us—suffer for us. Love that rejoices and welcomes us when we turn around and go back to Him.

THE WAY WE WERE MEANT TO LIVE

Come close to God, and God will come close to you.
- from JAMES 4:8 -

As I sat down to write this, the sun slipped lower in the winter sky trimmed with random, delicate wisps of clouds. At the edge of one gray strand, a short arc of rainbow appeared. I tried to take a photo, but the camera couldn't capture the ethereal beauty of that swatch of color against the blue of sky.

I feel a similar inadequacy as I write this. The hope we have of God's presence—the certainty of God being alive and with us in every moment of the day—is a hope to be celebrated and shared. And yet, how can words on a page capture the wonder and mystery of that? I know I cannot. I'll depend on God's words, not mine.

This is the secret of our lives now—our real lives: If we seek God, He comes close to us.

There it is. So simple. So life-changing.

We are not only invited to enter into the Holiest of Holies, but God comes to us.

- Jesus says that God the Trinity will come and make His home with each one who loves Him (John 14:23).

- "Look! I stand at the door and knock," says Jesus. "If you hear my voice and open the door, I will come in and we will share a meal together as friends" (Revelation 3:20). He's talking to a church, to people who claim to already know Him. Yet He's knocking, asking for further admittance into a closer, more intimate friendship.

- The Spirit of God lives in all those who believe Jesus is the Son of God. And those believers, in turn, "live in God" (1 John 4:13, 15).

- "Remain in me," Jesus says, "and I will remain in you. I'm the vine. You are the branches" (John 15).

- John wrote that as we live in God and God lives in us, our ability to love as He does grows more perfect (1 John 4:17).

- Christ makes his home in our hearts as we believe and trust in Him (Ephesians 3:17).

- Paul explains that our old selves have died on Christ's cross, and now "it is no longer I who live, but Christ lives in me" (Galatians 2:20).

- "And this is the secret: Christ lives in you" (Colossians 1:27).

Christ ripped apart the barrier between us and God. We no longer need special times and permission and conditions to enter His presence. Christ is now the priest who gives us access to the Almighty God. We step into God's presence, and He comes to live right here with us, within, living closer to us than even our spouses, our brothers and sisters, our closest friends.

He comes with intensity and intimacy. He shakes our lives.

He comes *in.* Because this is the way we were meant to live.

This is the secret of our new lives. It is the basis for making all things new, the basis of all the hope we are going to celebrate: We come close to God—we strive to live *in* Him, and He comes even closer to us.

And that makes all the difference.

WHY I MUST HAVE A RELATIONSHIP WITH MY CREATOR

Taste and see that the LORD is good. Oh, the joys of those who take refuge in him!

- **PSALM 34:8** -

So here is the question: Why does any of this matter? What difference does it make?

I can tell you what difference it has made, is making, and will forever make in my life.

I lived for many decades in fear of God—*fear,* as in being afraid, not fear in the Biblical sense of reverence and awe. I lived afraid of God— afraid of not being "good enough," afraid of the punishment I certainly deserved, afraid that I could never conquer the sinful part of me.

But even though I was afraid of God and His justice and judgment, I still made a pretty good mess of things.

Now I have lived the last three decades with this wonderful hope—a certainty that I am betting my life on—that I stand in God's presence without a single fault marked against me. He not only welcomes me, He lives with me and draws me into Him.

This hope, this certainty of my new standing with God, has changed my life—it gave me freedom. It constantly leads me "behind the curtain."

Why do I even care about coming into God's presence and being welcomed and accepted and loved?

Because I believe this is the way we were created to live.

Because it is the only way I *want* to live.

Because I believe God's purpose is to make everything new—and living a life of love and worship of the Creator is the only way we will be created anew.

And all of this is essential to my life because...?

Well, as the disciples said to Jesus, "Where else can we go? You are the one who has the words that will give us eternal life" (John 6:68).

This journey on earth is not our real life; we have a far greater life in a realm beyond what we can now see with our eyes. It's a life that goes on and on and on. It's life with heavenly privileges and powers. Jesus holds the keys and is the way to that existence.

And where else can I find hope? I've found nothing else that is certain in this world. I trust only the bridges of promise that God has laid before me.

So learning that I am now free to enjoy this relationship with my Creator—this is fantastic news! I no longer fear the wrath of God. Jesus provided the way for me to return to a bond of love that He has always desired to have with His creation.

And all the other hopes I've built my life upon come to fruition only within this relationship between God and those who love and worship Him.

Without that relationship with the Creator God, I cannot see any hope in this world. No hope for today or tomorrow—and certainly, no hope for my past.

But with God there is hope. So much hope!

To soak up more hope of new access to God,
see the appendix for a list of additional Scriptures.

**PRAYER FOR
ADOPTED CHILDREN:**

*Because of your unfailing love, I can
enter your house; I will worship at
your Temple with deepest awe.*

– **PSALM 5:7** –

NEW STATUS

 WHERE WE BELONG

But to all who believed him and accepted him, he gave the
right to become children of God.

– JOHN 1:12 –

"I don't know where I belong," she said. "I feel as though I don't fit anywhere."

I wasn't sure how to respond to that, because I knew exactly how she was feeling. I've felt it myself at times in my life.

How about you? Do you ever feel that you've

never found that exact niche where you fit perfectly? Yes, you may have made a place for yourself or taken the place assigned you in a family, a job, a church, a community, even a circle of friends. But do you ever long to find and be in the one place where you feel you were created to be, in a place where you fit perfectly?

You were created to be a child of God. You belong to Him.

I am overwhelmed when I think about the opening verse. Because I believe in Jesus Christ, I was given the *right* to become a child of God!

My identify, my self-image, my sense of worth, my entire perspective on my tiny pinpoint of life in this universe—all these things move to a different level with this one promise. I now have a new relationship with God. I am part of His family, a treasured child of the eternal Lord of the universe.

Child of God? Really? That's a big claim to make, I know.

Maybe you hesitate to call yourself a child of God because many people in the world today will think such a claim is pompous, outrageous, ridiculous, fanatic, and just downright crazy.

That's what the world will think. That's the way it will be. Those who don't believe in Christ will call us crazy fanatics.

But what does God say?

God says He rescued you in order to adopt you. It gave Him great pleasure to do that. You, His beloved child, are His treasure. And He has special privileges and a great inheritance for His children.

Once we get this into our heads and our hearts, we walk in a new life. It changes our perspective, our attitudes, our behavior, our hope, our view of ourselves, our view of the world. It changes everything.

If you've never thought of yourself as a child of God, take some time to step into your new identity.

- Read about what God says you are to Him (see the appendix).

- Change how you think about yourself by asking the Holy Spirit to give you that sense of new identity.

If you do believe that you are now a child of God, then take time to celebrate, and ask Him to open your eyes to all that He has for you, His beloved child. He always has so much more to show us!

IF YOU BELIEVE

He came into the very world he created, but the world
didn't recognize him. He came to his own people, and even
they rejected him. But to all who believed him and accepted
him, he gave the right to become children of God. They
are reborn—not with a physical birth resulting from human
passion or plan, but a birth that comes from God.

- JOHN 1:10-13 -

Have you ever wished you could begin a new life? That you could start over again, in a place where you have no history and have a chance to be a different person? Who or what would you want to be?

How about a new identity on a grand, eternal scale—one that will go on long after this life is over?

If you believe in the light and life that God sent into the world—Jesus Christ—then you have a new identity.

Your belief in Jesus brings you into God's family. The promises God makes to His children now belong to you. The privilege of worshiping Him, of knowing Him, of having His care and protection are yours. All of the hope that He lays before us is yours to claim.

Because you have been reborn. It isn't a human, earthly birth. God brings you alive to a new life, and in this new life, He is claiming you as His own child!

Who can do that? Who can be born to a new identity, to a new life, to a connection with the God of the whole universe?

Those who meet and believe in Jesus Christ.

That is what qualifies you to become a child of God. It is not dependent upon being "good enough." It's not a status you achieve or earn. It is not a destination at which you finally arrive. It does not depend on race or lineage, forefathers or tradition.

God is creating an entirely new kind of family and nation, but becoming a part of it depends on believing. God chooses to make you His son or daughter when you meet Christ and believe; you then become part of His people, those with whom He has a special relationship.

And He says to all who believe and accept, "You are now my beloved child. Come, and discover what I have for you."

 MOVING INTO THE PALACE

God sent [Christ] to buy freedom for us who were slaves to the law, so that he could adopt us as his very own children.

– **GALATIANS 4:5** –

Several years ago, for the very first time and in a condensed period of time, I read through the Bible chronologically. That intensive and sequential reading gave me a perspective on the complete story that I had never quite grasped before.

The history of this world is the story of the struggle between the Creator's good and His enemy's evil. And somewhere in this measure of time, each one of us plays his or her part in that battle.

The Old Testament stories are the same stories we live; the only difference is that they're set in other cultures and eras. In every time period, God rescues people from their slavery to move them out of the darkness and into His kingdom of light.

But He does not do this simply to claim trophies against the enemy. No, His purpose goes far deeper than that.

As the children of Israel were about to enter the Promised Land, Moses reminded them that God had rescued them from Egypt "in order to make you his very own people" (Deuteronomy

4:20). And then, many generations later, the apostle Paul wrote that we, too, were rescued from our slavery and brought to freedom "so that he could adopt us as his very own children" (Galatians 4:5).

He rescues us not only to free us, but to make us a part of Himself! To bring us back to Him and re-establish that perfect bond for which we were first created.

We are not His slaves or His soldiers. We are not accepted on a probationary basis. He creates between Himself and us a bond much more intimate, based not on the laws He gave but on His love and mercy. We belong to Him irrevocably, for all time.

There's great peace in knowing this. But in the last few years, as I've tried to make living as God's child a real part of my perspective and day-to-day life, I've seen that I had been living, instead, like a homeless child on the street—hungry, cold, and unaware of what life as a daughter of the King could actually be like.

But I've decided to move into the palace, and every day I want to learn more of how to live as the King's daughter!

The battle between God's justice and goodness and Satan's darkness and corruption goes on—every day, in every corner of the world.

It rages both within us and around us. But the final outcome is already settled.

The question before each of us today, this moment, is who we will be in the midst of this battle.

Will we live as God's enemy?

Or as His child, who yet wanders the streets like an orphan, with no idea of the life that is possible?

Or as His child, living in the castle as heir to the kingdom?

"WHAT HE WANTED TO DO"

God decided in advance to adopt us into his own family by bringing us to himself through Jesus Christ. This is what he wanted to do, and it gave him great pleasure.

– **EPHESIANS 1:5** –

I've caught a glimpse of the fierce desire that motivates adoption. I have not been an adoptive parent myself, but members of my family longed for and persistently pursued adoptions. Their deep desire to gather a child into their family caused them to pour their resources and lives into the process required to adopt.

Watching them and agonizing and praying with them as they persevered through many disappointments, I came to see more clearly the great lengths God went to in order to adopt me. How much He wants me as His child!

It gives God great pleasure to adopt us and declare us His children. The Almighty owns the universe—the sun and moon and stars, the seas and mountains, every tree and bird and creature—and yet, it is me and you that He treasures more than anything else.

Imagine. God reaches out and offers *His enemies* the opportunity to become a part of His family. It's what He wanted to do.

Instead of living in fear of His judgment and condemnation, we can live with privilege and hope as His children.

We have some long, cold winters here where I live. Even those of us who love the brilliant, brittle winter days eventually begin to hunger for longer hours of warm sunshine.

Sometimes life can seem stuck in a cold, hard season of winter, but even then you can bask in this sunshine: Claiming you as His child gives God great pleasure. His love treasures you above all else.

TWO THINGS TOO BIG FOR MY MIND

God, for whom and through whom everything was made,
chose to bring many children into glory. And it was only
right that he should make Jesus, through his suffering, a
perfect leader, fit to bring them into their salvation.
So now Jesus and the ones he makes holy have the same
Father. That is why Jesus is not ashamed to call them his
brothers and sisters.

- **HEBREWS 2:10-11** -

Do you suppose that someday, living in a world filled with peace and justice, with all of nature renewed and new bodies of our own and new perspectives on our earthly lives, we will look back and say, "If only I had known! If only I had understood more fully what God meant..."

Probably not. I doubt that we'll spend any time on regrets in our new heavenly life.

But I do think that we understand very little of what God intends for our lives when He names us His children.

My quest for hope, a study of Scriptures, had gone on for almost five years. But still I wanted to know: What does this really mean for my life today? What is the inheritance God speaks of giving to His children? What is the "glory" to which He brings His sons and daughters? What does it mean to live as a child of God?

And even many years later, I feel as if I've only just begun to understand. The plans God has for His children are plans on God's grand scale, not within our human limitations.

So I simply give you these Scriptures, and all I can say is that there is much here that is still beyond my imagination and understanding. I *want* to know more, though, because the glimpses I've had are exciting.

If you haven't already read the two verses opening this meditation, take a minute to do so now...

Astounding words! Here are the two things in particular that my mind tries to peer into—

God is bringing many children into glory. Don't you wonder what this glory is? We often refer to a home in heaven someday as "glory," but I believe it's so much more. I believe this glory also comes into this earthly life, here and now.

And Jesus is not ashamed to call us his brothers and sisters! Again, amazing. Do you ever think of Jesus Christ as a sibling? Jesus sees you in that way. I have no words to express my wonder over this.

It's obvious that God has big plans for those who believe and come to Him. It all begins when He makes us a part of His family.

Pondering these two things evokes our Psalm prayer, *Because of your unfailing love, I can enter your house; I worship You with deepest awe.*

 FOR EVERYONE

*And I tell you this, that many Gentiles will come from all
over the world—from east and west—and sit down with
Abraham, Isaac, and Jacob at the feast in
the Kingdom of Heaven.*

- **MATTHEW 8:11, JESUS SPEAKING** -

Matthew's story intrigues me. Many in his day called him *scum*.

When we first meet him, he's one of the hated tax collectors. Technically, he was a Jew. But he was looked upon as someone who was less than "acceptable" in Jewish society. He was piling up wealth by acting as the government's agent against his own people. *Traitor*, some would say.

Yet Jesus invited Matthew to become a follower. Matthew responded and apparently introduced Jesus to many of his friends and colleagues. Jesus came under sharp criticism for associating with this circle. In the eyes of "proper" Jewish folks, Matthew and his friends were all scum.

It's at this point that Jesus said, "That's who I'm here for. The sick. Those who know they need me."

As we read Matthew's Gospel, then, we read it knowing that this is an account written by an "outsider." When Matthew writes the story of his own calling and Jesus' response to the critics, his report is very personal. Because he knew he was one of those scum.

Following Jesus as a disciple, Matthew surely caught every syllable of the Teacher's words about coming to rescue the outcasts and the sick. Jesus was talking about *him*. And so it is Matthew also who caught and recorded Jesus' words that even the Gentiles—all those who were not originally part of God's chosen people—were going to be included in God's promises and blessing.

Jesus has opened the invitation to everyone.

No social, cultural, or economic restrictions limit this offer. Everyone who believes that Jesus is the Christ becomes a child of God (1 John 5:1). Anyone who wants to come can join God's household and family and have a seat at His table. The disciple John wrote of a prophecy that Jesus would die not only for the nation of Israel, but "to bring together and unite all the children of God scattered around the world" (John 11:52).

It's a new thing, this becoming a child of God. This new status makes you an heir to His promises and all that He has for His people. It's an amazing new relationship that God builds between Himself and the people who recognize and honor Him.

We can go forward into the unknown and

unseen future over this solid bridge of hope concerning our past: No matter who we once were, we now belong to the Father. And He has big plans for His children.

To soak up more assurance of your new status as a child of God, see the appendix for a list of additional Scriptures.

PRAYER FOR THOSE WANTING A NEW CONNECTION:

*My heart has heard you say, "Come and talk with me." And my heart responds, "L*ORD*, I am coming."*

– PSALM 27:8 –

NEW
CONNECTION
TO GOD

 THE NEW CONNECTION

You received God's Spirit when he adopted you as his own
children. Now we call him, "Abba, Father." For his Spirit
joins with our spirit to affirm that we are God's children.

- **from ROMANS 8:15-16** -

Union. Tie. Link. Coupling. Yoke. Affiliation.
Alliance. Relationship. Bond.

Those are all synonyms for the word
connection. None of those words are strong
enough, though, to describe the new connection

a person has with God when they are adopted as a son or daughter. None of those words conveys all the meaning of the amazing fact set out in Romans 8: *God not only adopts us, He plants His Spirit within us.*

John the Baptist preached that the coming Messiah would baptize with the Spirit. When Jesus prepared to leave this world, He said He would send the Holy Spirit to live with and in believers. And all through Acts and the early Christian letters, we read of the Holy Spirit dwelling within God's children.

As God is making all things new in the lives of His children, He gives each one a new connection to Him.

It may be difficult to believe that the Spirit of the Almighty God lives within *you.* That promise and hope might be hard to trust. It is quite a claim to make. And we might often not be able to feel the Spirit of God within. Maybe it's difficult to see any evidence of Him. Maybe it's just too crazy a concept to believe.

Maybe, at this point, all you can really say for certain is that you do believe the Bible is the Word of God and it is truth.

So let's take a look at what Scripture says about this new connection we have with God.

"WE'LL MAKE OUR HOME WITH YOU"

We will come and make our home with each of them.
— from JOHN 14:23 —

Have you ever had a dream crumble and disappear?

If so, you can understand the emotions of the twelve men who sat in disbelief as they listened to their leader's words.

They had turned their lives upside down just to join up with this man's team. Now he was simply going away. Where? They weren't exactly sure, but he said he was leaving. Why? They didn't have a clue. They could hardly take in what he was telling them. The dream of what they thought they had been building was cracking and crumbling. Imagine how they felt.

Then hear the tenderness in Jesus' voice as he watches their reactions and hears their confusion and anxiety. "I'm not abandoning you," He told them. "I won't leave you as orphans. I'll come to you."

They must have felt like orphans. Everything they had been trusting and counting on was slipping away.

"Don't be troubled," Jesus said. "Trust me. I will send you someone else. He'll never leave you, and He will be my representative, your comforter, advocate, and teacher."

Jesus repeats these things over and over in His final discussions with His disciples. He tries to reassure them. *Someone is coming who will never leave you; He will be all these things to you.*

The Creator is not a detached God who watches our struggles from afar and waits to judge us someday when we finally meet Him. He wants to be known *now*. That is what He wants more than anything else. He comes to those who love Him.

God has made this promise to every believer: His Spirit, the Spirit of Christ, will come and be a part of us. He gives us our new life. He takes up residence in our soul and connects us to God our Father.

I cannot explain how this happens. But I do know God promises this to His children. John wrote that everyone who declares that Jesus is the Son of God has "God living in them, and they live in God" (1 John 4:15). We may not be able to understand the *how* of our new connection to God, but that declaration gives us a hope we can trust.

And so I cross that bridge of promise and depend on the certainty of God living so intimately in my life that He is *in* me and will be my comforter, helper, and teacher.

 TO KNOW HIM BETTER

I keep asking that the God of our Lord Jesus Christ, the
glorious Father, may give you the Spirit of wisdom and
revelation, so that you may know him better.
- **EPHESIANS 1:17 (NIV)** -

Let's try to imagine what life in Eden must have been like. We can't really know, of course, but a few ideas do come to mind.

For one thing, I'd love to have life without snakes slithering about. And no weeds or thistles. No wardrobe worries. "Work" would have no connotations of difficulty or strain—work in Eden apparently did not involve the sweat and struggle. Most enviable of all—there's no guilt or fear. Adam and Eve enjoyed an intimate and free connection to their Creator without those barriers rising up between them. They knew Him as good friends know each other. The book of Genesis tells us, though, what happened to that perfect relationship.

As God makes all things new, He also re-establishes that special connection between Him and His new creations. His own breath first made man a living soul; now His Spirit, breathed into each of His children, gives us a new connection to Him. He gives us that Spirit not to enslave us but to share a close relationship with us (Romans

8:15-16). It is a sign of His love for us that the Spirit connects us to Him (Romans 5:5). He puts His Spirit in His children so that we can know him better.

The Lord of the universe, the Creator, wants us to know Him. He wants our hearts to know His love. He wants us to know that we are His children.

Does that warm your heart, as it does mine?

May our hearts hear, as our Psalm prayer says, our Father God saying, *Come. Come talk with me.*

KNOWING HIS SECRETS

For his Spirit searches out everything and shows us God's deep secrets. No one can know a person's thoughts except that person's own spirit, and no one can know God's thoughts except God's own Spirit. And we have received God's Spirit (not the world's spirit), so we can know the wonderful things God has freely given us.

- from 1 CORINTHIANS 2:10-12 -

"I'll tell you, but don't tell anyone. It's a secret."

Oh, the delicious delights of childhood friendship. Your friend always told *you*—and no one else—her secrets.

We grown-ups do the same thing, but in a

more adult way. Only a privileged few know our secrets.

That word *secret* seems to be a special key to friendship, and all of us have very old and deep emotional reactions to the word.

That's why it's rather startling to read the opening Scripture and find that the Spirit shows us *God's deep secrets.*

What? God tells His children His secrets?

Amazing.

In my Bible, the New Living Translation, there's an abridged "Word Study System" that looks at the meanings of the original Hebrew and Greek words. There I learn that the word *secrets* does not mean some knowledge that will be kept from all but a chosen few, like our treasured childhood secrets. It refers, instead, to things that have previously been hidden or unseen or unknown.

That's still a most amazing thing—that through His Spirit connecting us to Him, God shows us things we did not see or know before. The Spirit tunes us into God's thoughts and ways. He gives us understanding and insight that our earthly thinking could never grasp. He wants us to know all the wonderful things He has freely given us. He opens our eyes to see things that He is doing that we wouldn't otherwise be able to see or understand.

Yes, that is amazing.

And that Spirit is at work right now as you read and as you go forward through your day.

Even though God's thoughts and ways are so much higher than ours, He gives us this connection to Himself. He wants us to know Him. He wants us to understand what He is doing. And so His Spirit lives within, becomes a part of us, and breaks the barriers of our earth-bound minds.

That is very, very amazing.

"HE WILL..."

And I will ask the Father, and he will give you another Advocate, who will never leave you. He is the Holy Spirit, who leads into all truth.

– from JOHN 14:16-17 –

Jesus' life on the earth was God coming from eternal realms into our time and space. "If you see me and know me," Jesus said, "you have seen and know God."

I cannot explain the mystery of the Trinity, how God the Father, Jesus the Son, and the Holy Spirit are all somehow one. It is one of those bridges that I cross in faith as I go forward in my pilgrimage.

When Jesus spoke to His disciples about His coming death—and leaving them—He promised that instead of His human, physical presence, the Holy Spirit would come and live within every one of His disciples to continue His work. He emphasized this, repeating it again and again, to be certain they heard His assurance.

While we can't possibly cover in a few paragraphs everything the Spirit does in our lives, take a look at the conversation between Jesus and His disciples as He tries to prepare them for this new phase of His plan. In John 14:15-26 and 16:5-15, hear what Jesus promised the Spirit will do:

- "He will never leave you."

- "He will guide you into all truth."

- "He will be in you."

- "He will be my [Christ's] representative."

- "He will teach you everything."

- "He will remind you of everything I've told you."

- "He will convict the world of its sin."

- "He will tell you about the future."

- "He will bring me glory because He will pass on to you my truth and continue my teaching and my work."

Sometimes we've said or thought, "Oh, wouldn't it have been wonderful to live when Jesus was here on the earth..."

We are. He is.

Jesus didn't leave His followers as orphans. God doesn't leave us alone to muddle through.

His Spirit lives right here, within, making His home with every believer today. And He is also making good on all those "He will" promises that Jesus gave to every one of His disciples.

THE GUARANTEE

And as a guarantee he has given us his Holy Spirit.
- from 2 CORINTHIANS 5:5 -

Once upon a time, way back in my younger days, I wore a treasured locket. My parents gave it to me for Christmas one year. But it was particularly precious to me because my dad had picked it out—especially for me.

This may seem a simple thing to you, but understand, shopping for any kind of jewelry was completely out of my dad's comfort zone. I'm not sure he's ever done it since. And I know it probably happened that way at that Christmas time because Mom had dragged him along for shopping and asked his opinion. But still... Dad had picked it out. He had chosen this one for *me.*

No one else understood the worth of that locket to me, but every time I wore it, my heart glowed.

This new connection we have to God—doesn't it make your heart glow? God wants to live with you! Jesus wants to continue His work with *you* as His partner!

The Spirit living in me is like my heavenly Father's locket hanging round my neck.

It's a sign that I do indeed belong to Him:

And he has identified us as his own by placing the Holy Spirit in our hearts (from 2 Corinthians 1:22)

It's a guarantee that I can depend on all His promises:

[The gift of the Spirit is] the first installment that guarantees everything he has promised us. (2 Corinthians 1:22)

And it's even a promise of my future:

God himself has prepared us for this [eternal life with new bodies], and as a guarantee he has given us his Holy Spirit. (2 Corinthians 5:5)

God is serious about this connection between Him and His children. He wants His children to understand how committed He is to them. He's sealed His promises with His guarantee.

⫸ BRINGING US BACK ⫷

All of us must die eventually. Our lives are like water spilled out on the ground, which cannot be gathered up again. But God does not just sweep life away; instead, he devises ways to bring us back when we have been separated from him.

- **2 SAMUEL 14:14** -

Reading the Bible will destroy any image one might have of God as some omnipotent power, remote and uninvolved in our history and lives, simply letting us alone to muddle through.

The entire story of the Bible is the story of God constantly creating paths for His creation to come back to Him. Even when people aren't interested in knowing Him, He lays out possibilities and extends the invitation to enjoy a special connection with Him.

His purpose was for the nations to seek after God and perhaps feel their way toward him and find him—though he is not far from any one of us. (Acts 17:27)

And when our hearts hear Him say, "Come, and talk with me," may we respond, "Lord, I'm coming."

For more assurance that the Spirit of God lives in you, see the appendix for a list of additional Scriptures.

PRAYER FOR A NEW HEART:

Give me an undivided heart.

– from PSALM 86:11 (NIV) –

NEW HEART,
NEW CREATION

 **MASTERPIECE**

For we are God's masterpiece. He has created us anew in
Christ Jesus, so we can do the good things
he planned for us long ago.
— EPHESIANS 2:10 —

For a long time, I thought being a Christian was all about what I did and what I made of myself: I must do this, I must not do that; I've got to be more of this, less of that; I need to get rid of my old selfish way of thinking and create a new me that lines up with what God wants.

But I was a colossal failure at producing a life that spread God's grace and love. Doing it on my own was hopeless. I could only take comfort in Psalm 103:13-14: God loves me, but He knows how weak I am, that I am "only dust." I was counting on God's mercy for all my failures.

I had not yet learned this amazing promise of God: that He can take this dust and create something new and extraordinary.

From the dirt under His feet, He made human bodies so complex that even now, with all our science and technology, we do not fully understand them. For all of my life, I have believed in the Creator. But now I am learning something new about my Creator—that God has taken this flimsy cloud of dust (me!) and is in the process of creating something He calls *masterpiece.*

That's a pretty big jump, isn't it? Can we go from realizing and acknowledging how undeserving we are of *any* attention from the God of the universe to saying that we are becoming His masterpiece?

Yet that is what God says about those who come to Him. The only requirement is that we come and believe, and then He adopts us, gives us a new life, and goes about creating a new you, a new me. His plans for us go far beyond what we can imagine.

While this new life we've been given exists on a level beyond the earthly, God also works with our very earthly hearts and minds and bodies (and situations) to transform our lives here on earth.

He did not give us new life just as a "do over" or a second chance. His plans are to make us completely new people, living out that new life.

This is not a promise for a far-off day when we're perfect in paradise. God is even now creating the new you and the new me, creating us to be and to do what He intended.

This hope is so startling and so immense that even those of us who claim it will never comprehend it all while we are here on earth. But let's at least begin to think about this new creation of... *us*. Let's ask our Father for just a few tantalizing and exciting glimpses into what He has planned. Let these glimpses change our thinking about ourselves, our past failures, and what we now are to God.

Today, ponder these words applied to you (yes, you!): *Created anew and a masterpiece.*

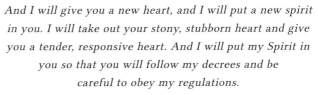

CAN A LEOPARD CHANGE ITS SPOTS?

*And I will give you a new heart, and I will put a new spirit
in you. I will take out your stony, stubborn heart and give
you a tender, responsive heart. And I will put my Spirit in
you so that you will follow my decrees and be
careful to obey my regulations.*

— **EZEKIEL 36:26-27** —

Do people ever change? Can people change?
I'm sure you've heard it said (usually accompanied
with a sad shake of the head), "A leopard never
changes its spots."

Here's some good news: God can and will
change your spots.

Those things that *you* can never change? God
says He can and He will make you into a new
person. Hope knows that God is able to do what
He says He will do.

The passage above from Ezekiel is a message
from God to the wayward nation of Israel.
They were far from God, and the evil way they
were living was far from what God wanted His
people to be on the earth. Yet, even though they
did not deserve any of God's favor, He promised
to restore them. He promised to wash away
their filth, make them new, and give them new
lives and new hearts. Later in the same chapter,
God said He would turn a wasteland into the
Garden of Eden, and everyone would know it

could only have been God who had done this (see verses 35-36).

This is the entire story of the Bible—God changing our wasteland into a Garden of Eden. God making us new people. He makes the same promise today: He will change us, and give us new hearts and spirits.

Before we go any further, each one of us must make a decision: Are we going to believe what human nature tells us, or are we going to believe what the Almighty Creator says is reality in His kingdom where we now live?

In chapter 37 of Ezekiel, the prophet tells about going to a valley where bones were scattered everywhere, dried by the sun and picked clean by the vultures. Those naked, bleached bones represented Israel, God's people. The people knew their plight, how dead they were. They were saying "We have become old, dry bones—all hope is gone" (Ezekiel 37:11).

"What do you think?" the Lord asked Ezekiel, as he surveyed the valley of death. "Could these bones ever be living people again?"

Is there any hope?

Looking at such a scene, we'd probably all be doubtful. Ezekiel's reply sounds doubtful, too. I wonder if he was thinking that he wanted to believe... he really should believe... but yet...

"Only you know that, Lord," he finally replied.

How will you answer the Lord if He asks you, "Do you believe what is dead in you can live again? Do you believe I can cleanse your heart and create a new spirit in you? Do you believe I can create a new *you?*"

Only You can do that, Lord.

And what was the end of the dry-bones story?

The Spirit of the Lord put flesh and muscle on those bleached, dried bones, covered them with skin, and gave them breath. An army came to life, living people, rising up and walking around Ezekiel. Whether this was a vision or it actually happened, Ezekiel must have been shaken by the sight.

God's message to Israel was this: You are not without hope. I will put my Spirit in you, you will live, and you will know that I have done it.

This is God's message for us, too.

There is hope for leopards. God says He will change our spots. And it will be so remarkable, we will know that it could only have been the Almighty doing it.

This was His purpose in rescuing and adopting us—to create new hearts and spirits within us, to bring alive His new creation.

When we step onto this bridge of hope and go forward, trusting it to carry us, it changes everything as we travel the road ahead.

HIS PLAN TO CHANGE THOSE WHO SEEK HIM

I will give them hearts that recognize me as the LORD. They will be my people, and I will be their God, for they will return to me wholeheartedly.

— JEREMIAH 24:7 —

Tenacity is required when reading through the Old Testament. Many parts—sometimes entire books—are difficult to get through, especially if you have no idea of the context of certain passages. But when you read it according to a chronological sequence, one thing becomes very clear: God's purposes have always been to restore and renew His creation and His people.

The Creator had initiated a special covenant relationship with the descendants of Abraham. Countless times, these people turned away from Him and decided they wanted nothing to do with Him. Usually, that brought disaster, even a destruction of their homeland and exile into foreign countries.

Yet the promise of the Father was always the same: *If you seek me, I'll be found. I'll restore you and heal you.* The opening verse from Jeremiah contains God's word to His people while they were still living in exile in a foreign country that had conquered them.

He promised them new hearts.

Further, He said, He would watch over them (v.6), build them up, not tear them down, plant them, and not uproot them.

Whatever our circumstances, even when it seems God is not hearing our prayers or has shut us out of His presence—even then!—He is watching over His children and has plans to restore and heal them.

If we pray for a heart to recognize, worship, and love God, He honors those prayers. He has said, "Draw near to me, and I'll draw near to you. Seek me, and you'll find me."

Here's one more promise, given to the exiles but also for each of us today:

They will be my people, and I will be their God. And I will give them one heart and one purpose: to worship me forever, for their own good and for the good of all their descendants. (Jeremiah 32:38-39)

This is God's long-term plan: To make everything new, including the hearts of His people. We can boldly ask Him for this, because it is a promise for each of us, too. He will give a new heart and new purpose.

And we will find that worshiping Him will be "for our own good"—and the good of our descendants!

〜〜 CHANGING OUR THINKING 〜〜

Don't copy the behavior and customs of this world, but let
God transform you into a new person by changing the way
you think. Then you will learn to know God's will for you,
which is good and pleasing and perfect.

– **ROMANS 12:2** –

I do not want to do this, I thought as I drove down the street.

I knew exactly how the meeting would go. It was a pattern we had followed over the better part of our friendship. I knew what he would say. I knew how I would react. The ending was never good. And the ending was never *God.*

Do you notice the one word that starts most of those sentences and thoughts? (Hint: The word has one letter.)

Still driving, I remembered this section I was then working on for this book—*A new heart. A new creation. Promised by the heavenly Father.* Yes. That's exactly what I needed in this situation.

Father, help! I prayed. *I need a new heart. Change my thinking and feeling about this.*

The conversation with my friend that day was a completely new one, with a completely different outcome.

An explanation of the change in me—and thus in the situation—is not possible, except to say that somehow God changed the 'I' factor. And the ending was good. The ending was God.

How do we change our thinking? How do we keep the behavior and attitudes of this world from soaking into us? We're blasted by the media, advertising, cultural values, and all those insistent voices around us. How do we keep those voices from shaping our thinking?

We don't.

Did you notice what the Scripture says?

"Let God transform you by changing the way you think."

God is the one who is changing us into masterpieces; it is His work that transforms us. Our efforts will always fall short. We can never create new hearts and minds on our own.

We must, however, be willing to let Him work.

There are many ways God works to change and mold us into new persons. We'll look at some of those ways. But sometimes, it really is an instant miracle, brought about by a plea for help—help that only God can provide. I think that's what happened to me that night.

The only explanation I can offer is that this is part of our hope: God is ready, willing, and able to change us when we call to Him for help. And sometimes, it is only by a miracle and nothing else.

 WHITTLING

And I am certain that God, who began the good work
within you, will continue his work until it is finally
finished on the day when Christ Jesus returns.

- PHILIPPIANS 1:6 -

The Scripture uses a variety of metaphors to describe how God creates us anew. We'll look at many of them at different times in this study. Let's ponder a word that comes, not from the Scriptures, but from a friend.

In response to my thoughts on being thankful for the difficult in our lives, a friend's comments included this line: "A whittling down of ourselves to make us what we need to be."

Whittle. That's a fascinating word. It immediately brings up a related word: *carve.*

Think of the words we pair with those two.

We *whittle away* or *whittle down.* Skilled fingers take a piece of wood and cut away a bit here and a chunk there until, eventually, they hold a work of art. We even use this phrase to describe working, bit by bit, at a large project. We whittle away at it; and eventually—the finished result!

We *carve out.* Sculptors are sometimes quoted as saying they see what is in a piece of marble or a slab of wood before they even start their work. Carving is a prying away of unnecessary, inessential, inappropriate, and irrelevant material —until the image the creator has "seen" finally emerges.

Isn't that the way God forms and molds us? He is at work, whittling away the things in our lives that need to go in order for His masterpiece to finally emerge. "Whittling down of ourselves to make us what we need to be."

We were created in the image of God! (No matter how many times I type that, I am still amazed at the words.) But as sons and daughters of Adam and Eve, we've inherited so much that sullies and burdens and binds and tarnishes that image. We've taken on selfishness and disobedience and pride. All of us were trained as citizens of the kingdom of darkness instead of sons and daughters in the kingdom of light.

Yet God's promise is that we are now His masterpiece, created anew.

There are many days I don't feel like a masterpiece of any kind, let alone a masterpiece of the great Creator. But this word *whittling* has opened a new thought for me: God is whittling away at this chunk of wood I know as Me. He sees the image within; He knows what He has created there (a new person, with a new life born of His Spirit), and He is carving out that image, bit by bit cutting away everything else.

And that is exactly why we can be thankful in all things, even the difficult and trying and painful. God promises that He is at work on His new creation within us. He knows what He intends to make us. He knows what needs to go.

He whittles away all the old stuff that Self has collected, so that the new life He has given us can grow and thrive.

He'll keep whittling, the Scripture says, until finally the masterpiece emerges.

CLEANSING

If we confess our sins to him, he is faithful and just to forgive us our sins and to cleanse us from all wickedness.
— 1 JOHN 1:9 —

Here's a word of hope that I am counting on: *Cleansing.*

I often feel the need of a cleansing, a deep cleaning that I cannot accomplish on my own. Oh, yes, I've tried scrubbing some things out of my life, but stubborn streaks still there require a greater power.

(Okay, I admit it. Instead of using the phrase *stubborn streaks,* I should have used *wickedness.* That's much more accurate.)

This opening verse from the apostle John may have been one of the first scriptures you learned as a little child. It promises that God is always ready and willing to forgive us when we confess our failings.

But there's so much more than forgiveness promised here. I missed it for years, because I was focused on the needed forgiveness. But did you see that last phrase? *And to cleanse us from all wickedness.*

Wow.

It turns out that this promise is not just a simple little formula for ridding ourselves of guilt of our wrongdoing. John is not teaching confession only for the purpose of obtaining forgiveness.

As we look further into this promise, we discover that going to God and confessing our sins will actually further His "cleansing" of us. He works at purging and purifying those parts of us that need to go.

We may have created a mess today with poor or immoral choices, and when we confess, God forgives that, yes. But *cleansing* goes deeper: When we live in His light and admit to those things in our lives that the light shows to be wrong, God promises to be at work, scrubbing and cleaning us! He is not only forgiving our disobedience and forgetting it, but He is also cutting away our old wayward and rebellious nature and replacing it with something brand new.

This is such good news for me.

When we go to God in confession, He does something we can never accomplish on our own. His power works through our confession to weaken the grip our old self has on us. He is cleaning the old life right out of us.

This is part of our hope of new creation—a deep, necessary cleansing!

 **CREATED TO BE LIKE GOD**

Put on your new nature, created to be like God—
truly righteous and holy.
- EPHESIANS 4:24 -

Do you think that title is just a little too daring?

The thoughts on the next few pages are pretty hard to swallow for those who don't believe the Word of God. And even when we have determined to set our course by His Word, this is all still a mystery—the mystery of God's relationship with His sons and daughters. We haven't even begun to plumb the depths of this hope.

But standing firm in this hope and believing what God says is true will completely change how we look at ourselves and at our brothers and sisters in Christ's kingdom.

Ephesians 4 encourages us to put on the new nature that God gave each of us. This new nature was "created to be like God" (See verse 24).

His purpose is to change us, every day, bringing more and more of His own character into full bloom in our lives, until our mortal dust is swallowed up by His immortal character and glory.

Paul wrote in 2 Corinthians 3:18 that the Spirit is changing us to be more and more like Christ. The Greek word translated as *changed* means *to change fundamentally and completely from one state to another.*

Amazing. Changed from *me* to *Him.*

Are you thinking the same things I've thought or said myself? Thoughts like, "I am so far from being God's masterpiece. I'd like to think of myself that way, but those old, ugly habits still rise up too often. I have those days when I am everything but holy. I am so far from what God wants me to be."

And sometimes we even think, "I'm hopeless. I'll never get this right."

Yet this is God's promise: the old can be

gone. The new has come. And the new nature He created in us was created to be like Him. The Spirit is working to make us "more and more like Him."

That's amazing. And such good news!

This means there's hope for me—even on those days when I feel "hopeless."

Because the life I'm living now was birthed by God. He's nurturing it and has big plans for my new life.

Is it so hard to believe that the Spirit of Christ changes us to be like Him? We accept that this happens on a human level. Within hours of a child's birth, people are looking for Daddy's dimples or Mom's eyes or Big Sister's nose. We take it further than the physical; we say that "He has his dad's business savvy" or "She's got her grandfather's gumption" or "She inherited her mother's sweet disposition."

This birth of a new nature in us was a birth from God, and He birthed His character in us. That's a pretty daring thing to say, isn't it? Yet there it is in God's Word to tell us exactly what He has planned.

Peter wrote that the great and precious promises God has given us "enable you to share his divine nature and escape the world's corruption caused by human desires" (2 Peter 1:4).

Apparently God doesn't just change the leopard's spots, the outward appearance. He changes our very being.

Yes, He birthed His character in us when He gave us this new life. It's a bold statement; many will think it's too extreme and fanatical. But there it is, in His Word to us. It's part of His plan to turn us into His true sons and daughters.

GLORY... IN US

And the Lord—who is the Spirit—makes us more and more like him as we are changed into his glorious image.
- from 2 CORINTHIANS 3:18 -

Would you say that radiance, splendor, importance, power, and wondrous beauty are found in *you?*

Ever since 2 Corinthians 3:18 began soaking into my head, I have been in awe of the truth that God is changing all of His children to reflect His glory.

Amazing.

He created us in His image to begin with, then we pretty much ruined it, and now His purpose is to restore us to that image that shines with His own glory.

This has completely changed my former thoughts about glory.

First, I always thought the attribute of *glory* belonged to God alone, but there's a long list of Scriptures that tell us it is meant for us to share, too.

My NLT Word Study System says the Greek word used here and translated as *glory* is a noun meaning "radiance or splendor, with a strong association of importance or display of power. It refers to eye-catching, wondrous beauty, perhaps with a focus on the object shining or reflecting light. Glory means ascribing honor or praise, emphasizing that the person being honored is powerful, beautiful, important."

Glory. His glory. In ever increasing measure. In us!

Second, my idea of the glory awaiting followers of Jesus was that it was some reward in heaven, when we will be transformed and made perfect. But this is His plan for us *now*—we *"are being transformed* into his image with ever increasing glory, which comes from the Lord." (That's the NIV translation of the opening verse. The italics are mine.)

Here's another glimpse: "And this is the secret: Christ lives in you. This gives you assurance of sharing his glory" (Colossians 1:27).

The Spirit of Christ that brought you a new life is the One who is now transforming you into His image. The book of Hebrews says the Son "radiates God's own glory and expresses the very character of God" (Hebrews 1:3). And we have that very Spirit of the Son living in us!

In 1 Corinthians 2:9, the apostle Paul quotes Scripture from Isaiah:

No eye has seen, no ear has heard,
and no mind has imagined what God has
prepared for those who love him.

I can't imagine what all He must have planned for His children. I'm still struggling to grasp the fact that here and now, in this world, God is already changing me to be like Christ and filling me with *His glory.*

Those WWJD bracelets seemed like a good idea to remind us who we follow, but I have to admit that often I'm stumped at answering the question, *What would Jesus do in this situation?* For me, the answer's not always clear.

So I'm still learning, and I'm walking ahead over the bridge of this promise: God is changing me to be more like Him and continuing to create a new nature in me.

Scripture assures us that the more we get to know our Creator, the more His power transforms us.

Right now, He's creating a new me. Even though I'm sometimes stubborn or foolish or a slow learner, He's continuing to create me to be His child, in His image.

And your hope can know that whatever you've done, whatever you've been in the past, God has promised to make you a new creation.

For more of God's promise to create a new you,
see the appendix for a list of additional Scriptures.

**PRAYER TO REMIND US
WHERE WE LIVE:**

*Your kingdom is an everlasting
kingdom. You rule throughout all
generations.*

– **from PSALM 145:13** –

NEW REALM
OF LIVING

SETTING OUR SIGHTS

For [God] has rescued us from the kingdom of darkness
and transferred us into the Kingdom of his dear Son, who
purchased our freedom and forgave our sins.

- COLOSSIANS 1:13-14 -

Call me a dinosaur in this techie age, if
you will, but I continue to be fascinated by
the accuracy and detail of the GPS app on my
smartphone.

This little gadget knows exactly where I am.

When the screen says I'm crossing Smith Road, I glance at the street sign and see—sure enough!—"Smith Road." Switching views, I can have a birds-eye view of trees and buildings along my route. Even when I have to back up or pull a U-turn, that little arrow mimics every movement of my car.

And if I suspend the tracking for a time and then come back to the app, all I need to do is push *Resume*, and zip! In a second, that omniscient arrow is back on track, telling me exactly where I am and in what direction I'm headed.

I wish I had a *Resume* button on my spiritual sights.

Since Jesus rescued each one of us, we're living in new territory. We must not forget that.

After God had rescued the Israelites from slavery in Egypt, He told them, "You saw what I did to the Egyptians. I carried you on eagles' wings and brought you to myself. Worship me, obey my laws, be my own special people, a nation I've chosen and set apart for myself" (see Exodus 19:3-6).

That's what God has done and promised for everyone who believes in Christ. Jesus came right into the dark domain ruled by Satan and ransomed us, so that we could be a part of His Kingdom instead. He carried us to Himself, to become His own special people.

So now, even though we're still living on this earth, we're living lives that belong to a new world, a new realm, a new nation, a new kingdom.

We are living lives that belong to a new reality, a heavenly, spiritual realm.

When Jesus started his public speaking, He began talking about the good news of the Kingdom. The message was this:

- God is establishing a new kingdom on earth,

- a kingdom not structured on earthly principles or according to human logic,

- not limited by what we think possible or practical,

- not governed or restricted by this world's values, rules, or rewards.

- This kingdom is ruled by God's power and grace,

- and His plans for His creation and His people.

There are now heavenly dimensions to our lives on this earth, and, writes Paul, this new life is our "real" life, so we need to keep our perspective on the realities of heaven (see Colossians 3:1-3).

Too often, I forget. I forget the truths

of Christ's Kingdom, *the facts* under God's everlasting rule. My thinking stays bound in its earthly habits. I lose sight of the truths in this realm where I've been given a life.

That's when I need a spiritual *Resume* button—to zoom me back to a proper orientation and perspective of where I'm now living—in a new kingdom, in a new life, with new realities.

The Psalm prayer for this week can serve as that reorientation button. Short and simple, the line acknowledges God's everlasting sovereignty and reminds us that this is where we're now living—in the realities of God's Kingdom.

NEW THINKING IN THIS NEW REALM

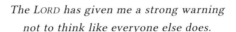

The LORD has given me a strong warning
not to think like everyone else does.

- from ISAIAH 8:11 -

Judah was about to be invaded. War was imminent. The prophets were issuing warnings from God that the country would be crushed. The picture was grim: their society was filled with evil, injustice, and corruption, and the future held only darkness, distress, and captivity.

And then the prophet Isaiah received this word from the Lord:

The LORD has given me a strong warning not to think like everyone else does. He said, "Don't call everything a conspiracy, like they do, and don't live in dread of what frightens them. Make the LORD of Heaven's Armies holy in your life. He is the one you should fear. He is the one who should make you tremble. He will keep you safe." (Isaiah 8:11-14)

I find that passage so interesting. It could be written directly to us today, living in a world of turmoil, evil, fear, and uncertainty. For us today, it would say:

But don't think like everyone else does! Instead, look higher than man. God is the one who holds your future. He is the one who should command fear and trembling. He alone is the one who keeps you safe. Man is nothing compared to the Lord of Heaven's Armies!

When we think about our lives, is our thinking caught and limited by what's going on in this worldly kingdom? How does the evening news affect us? What will happen if the "wrong" candidate wins the next election? Do we worry about that? Do we believe that our future depends solely on what happens here at earth level?

Do we think like the world—believing that everything depends on this human race and what it can or cannot accomplish? Or do our sights go higher than the human arena?

Your life now, child of God, is part of something much more than the country, state, community, and culture in which you live your earthly days.

Jesus said His kingdom is now here. It is not something we wait for, something we hope will arrive someday. We are a part of His kingdom now. We can look beyond what's going on in our society and our government to glimpse the kingdom in which we live as people chosen and adopted by the Lord of the universe. We are now citizens of a kingdom that goes so far beyond this earth that it has no end.

Just as surely as King David and Jesus' mother, Mary, and the apostle Paul are part of God's story, *so are we.* We are living out the history of the kingdom of God right now.

Can we stop thinking like the world around us and ask God to give us a glimpse of His thoughts?

Let's make it more personal and specific, with one example. A few pages ago, we meditated on the promises of a new nature and new heart. As you read, did you ever find yourself thinking, *Yes, but...?* We're so conditioned to think like the world and say, "Let's be realistic. This part of me will never change." But God doesn't want us to think like everyone else. He wants us to ground our thinking in the realities of His realm. And one of those realities is the promise that He is creating us anew, changing us to be His sons and daughters. His power is able to do things far beyond anything we can even imagine.

Earth-thinking shackles us with lies; it keeps us earth-bound. Once our sights shift to heaven's realities, our thinking changes, too, and our eyes begin to see what living can be like in this realm of God's Kingdom.

THE LIVING WE'RE CALLED TO

Don't repay evil for evil. Don't retaliate with insults when
people insult you. Instead, pay them back with a blessing.
That is what God has called you to do,
and he will bless you for it.

- 1 PETER 3:9 -

A man shoots ten young Amish girls. Five of the girls die. Amish and non-Amish alike, families of the children and families of the murderer, the entire community—all are ripped open by the killer's brutal actions. Yet the Amish say, "We will forgive."

God says, "Do not repay evil for evil. Love those who hate you. Bless those who curse you. Pray for those who work against you. Offer the other cheek also."

While I am asking God to show me what turning the other cheek means, a friend tells me her story.

Her summer home is somewhat secluded, and while she was away during the winter, someone broke in and stole a number of things. She knew who had done it, yet she did not accuse; the young man already had a record, but she did not file a report with authorities. She tried to see the young man as Jesus saw him, and wanted to loved him as Jesus loved him.

The end of the story? She let the young man know he must return her things. He did bring back what he still had in his possession, and, that fall as she prepared to leave, he agreed to send her monthly installments to reimburse her for what he had already sold. "And it came to me to ask him to watch my house that winter, which he did! By the next spring, all was repaid." They became and remained good friends for as long as they were both in the same neighborhood, and, as far as she knows, he mended his ways and "went straight" after that.

"Turning the other cheek," my friend says,

"is seeing others as God sees them."

What is going on in these two stories? How can people so wronged not want revenge? How can someone give the guilty a second and third and fourth chance to inflict harm?

This is living in a realm other than this world. These people have been called into a new kind of living.

Blessing for insult. Good for evil. Forgiveness and turning the other cheek. Jesus Christ blazed a new way of life for His followers. He preached and patterned a new way of living, one with standards dramatically contradictory to the attitudes and actions of his day—and to those of our day, too.

We are no longer a part of this world. We are citizens of a different kingdom. And in Jesus' kingdom, we're shedding our old ways of thinking and acting and being, and we're putting on the new.

Colossians 3 says that as God's people we must clothe ourselves with tenderhearted mercy, kindness, humility, gentleness, and patience. Forgive others, and—above all—wrap it all in love.

I can spend far too much time in front of the closet deciding how to clothe my body for the day. I want to spend more time with my Heavenly Father, learning how to prepare for my day by putting on the wardrobe above—a wardrobe appropriate for His daughter.

Sometimes we say that when Jesus came along teaching about the Kingdom of Heaven, He turned things upside down with His new guidelines for thinking and acting. Isn't it more accurate to say that His Kingdom turns things right side up again?

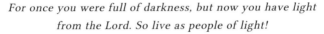

THE KINGDOM ON EARTH

For once you were full of darkness, but now you have light from the Lord. So live as people of light!

– **EPHESIANS 5:8** –

Jesus announced that the Kingdom of Heaven was invading the earthly realm. Our lives now have heavenly dimensions, and we are to be living out Christ's kingdom, right now, right here.

Jesus' way is so different from the ways of this world, and the "laws" of our new kingdom are so different from those of the world. In this heavenly realm:

- God's plans and power rule.

- Weakness makes place for God's strength,

- the meek inherit the earth,

- suffering produces good,

- mercy replaces condemnation,

- selfish ambition gives way to a life of serving others,

- giving up your life means you will find it,

- and being last makes you great.

God asks us, as His children and citizens of heaven, to order our lives quite differently than the world would recommend. We are to:

- Love Him above all else,

- forgive,

- pray for our enemies,

- give up what the world considers our "rights,"

- put others before ourselves,

- make Kingdom matters more important than earthly matters,

- depend on God to take care of us rather than relying on our own wits and power,

- seek treasures in heaven instead of on earth.

The world will see this way of living as foolish, ridiculous, weak, or stupid. But the results and effects, blessings and rewards, of living under

God's rule are also quite different than the world would imagine or expect.

This is the hope we are basing our lives on: We do not belong to and are not limited by this world. We belong to Christ's kingdom, where God's righteousness rules and His truth and plans will prevail.

WHEN THE WORLD HATES US

If the world hates you, remember that it hated me first. The world would love you as one of its own if you belonged to it, but you are no longer part of the world.

— **JOHN 15:18-19a** —

It's easy enough to write all this from the privacy and comfort of my living room couch. But while we are living in God's Kingdom, we are still also residents in the domain of God's enemy, and every day we come into conflict with that world and all its forces.

Listen to the words of Jesus, warning His disciples of what was coming:

In this world you will have trouble. (John 16:33 NIV)

And everyone will hate you because you are my followers. (Luke 21:17)

When people mock you, lie about you,
and say evil things about you because you
are my followers... (Matthew 5:11)

The time is coming when those who
kill you will think they are doing a holy
service for God. (John 16:2)

We are living in such times, too.

Every day, we must make the choice of whose
standards we're going to live by and who we're
going to bow to as ultimate authority. God's plan
is for us to show His way of living; we're to be
planted in and permeating a world of darkness.
But every single one of the attitudes and actions
that Jesus teaches will come into conflict with the
values, the strategies, and the goals of the world.

And the kingdom of darkness brings everything
against us in its war against God's Kingdom:

- family or friends who ridicule our values

- those who call us "haters" and "bigots" for
  proclaiming truth

- a coworker who lies to make me look
  bad, a friend angry when I refuse to go
  along with a questionable plan, a school
  or library trying to force us to expose
  our children to certain material, a fellow
  church member sowing discontent

- a government that passes laws making it illegal to live out our beliefs
- people who want to kill us because we bear the name of Christ

The list could go on and on... you may already know where, today, the kingdom of Satan will come against you because you belong to the Kingdom of Heaven. And sometimes, the enemy attempts to ambush us.

As we face these attacks, remember the One who rescued us and brought us to live in His kingdom.

Jesus knows what every one of us faces. He knew it all long ago. He knew what people would say to and about us. He knew what they would do to us. He knew our need for bravery and courage and reassurance. He knew what attacks by evil forces would come against us.

He prayed for us. When agonizing over His own battle with evil and knowing He was going to die—He took the time to pray for every one of us who decides to follow Him (John 17.) And He is still going to the Father on our behalf.

Nothing will happen to me or you today that He does not know about.

Nothing will happen that He will not use for our good and the mission of His Kingdom on earth.

And nothing will happen that He will not be right there, with us.

When we come face-to-face with a world that hates us, these are all promises we can count on, realities of His kingdom.

WITH OUR EYES ON THE UNSEEN

For the things we see now will soon be gone, but the things we cannot see will last forever.
– from 2 CORINTHIANS 4:18 –

Consider how Moses handled opposition.

Could there be a more formidable earthly opponent than the mighty pharaoh of Egypt? He was a ruler who considered himself a god, and he looked at a group of people in his country who were living in a choice part of the land, doing well, flourishing, and becoming quite prosperous and powerful. "Enough of this," he thought, and with his political and social manipulation, Jacob's descendants suddenly found their idyllic life in Egypt was over. They were slaves, with a king who was killing their babies and cutting off the hands of people who did not produce enough.

It's no wonder, then, that Moses needed a great deal of convincing to accept God's command to go and face this opponent. Yet once he accepted the mission, he never stopped, no matter what Pharaoh threw at him.

> It was by faith that Moses left the land of Egypt, not fearing the king's anger. He kept right on going because he kept his eyes on the one who is invisible.
> (Hebrews 11:27)

Isn't that an interesting combination of words? Moses kept his eyes (seeing) on the one who is invisible (something that can't be seen).

Paul uses the same combination when he says "we fix our gaze on things that cannot be seen" (2 Corinthians 4:18).

How do we fix our gaze on something that can't be seen?

Apparently, there are two kinds of sight: Eyes that see things we touch and eat and feel. And eyes of faith, that can see invisible things that last forever.

If you look at the context of these two verses, the writers are saying that this is what keeps us going through our troubles. This is how we cope with earthly life. This is what keeps us strong through rough waters—keeping our eyes on the invisible.

Because we know the invisible will last forever.

So we keep our eyes on the realities of the unseen Kingdom where we're now living, and we keep right on going.

≈ EXTREME PROMISE ≈

Seek the Kingdom of God above all else, and live righteously, and he will give you everything you need.
- **MATTHEW 6:33** -

These words of Jesus must have been just as shocking and extreme to His original listeners as they are to us today. In every era that God's children have lived on this earth as strangers and pilgrims, they have sought to understand and live the depth of these words. I believe we will never exhaust the limits of this promise, delivered in the words of Jesus.

Jesus has just declared that we do not need to worry about food and clothes. What? These are basic necessities of life!

God knows everything you need, Jesus said, and He will provide it. Don't worry about those things. Make it your #1 goal to seek the Kingdom. This Kingdom we live in now is more important than anything in our physical, earthly lives.

This is hard to understand, and even harder to live out. I have all kinds of questions for my Lord.

But I trust His character. He knows everything about me, right down to a few strands of hair falling out as I brush, and I believe He keeps all His promises. He has, from the beginning of time, cared for His children like a shepherd protects and cares for His sheep. I claim Psalm 23. In the care of my Shepherd Father, I want for nothing.

When it comes to living on this promise, I don't doubt God—I doubt me.

How do I put the Kingdom of God and His purposes at the top of my priorities, to such an extent that I can live without worrying about what we call the basics of life? Yes, my faith is so little. I *want* to give all of myself, but I have a constant battle trying to keep earthly things in their proper place and perspective.

Yet the promise is there. The bridge that keeps me moving forward is the promise that God will take care of my needs as I strive to live as a citizen of the Kingdom of Heaven.

And I believe God keeps His promises and does not lie. So I continue seeking to let go of the things that I worry about and seeking to find one more way I can be living in the invisible Kingdom right now.

 WHAT WE HAVE COME TO

*Since we are receiving a Kingdom that is unshakable, let us
be thankful and please God by worshiping him
with holy fear and awe.*

– HEBREWS 12:28 –

And what does all this mean? If we've been
given a life in the Kingdom of Heaven, a life in
the invisible realm of the eternal, where do we
find ourselves?

The writer of Hebrews lays out this hope so
beautifully. Read the following, taken from Hebrews
12, and visualize yourself in this new place God has
brought you to. (I've paraphrased slightly.)

> When you come to the Kingdom of God,
> you do not come to a life rooted in the
> earthly world, to an unapproachable God,
> or to demands for holiness that cannot be
> achieved.

> No, you've come to the city of the living
> God, and to a joyful gathering of the
> angels.

> You've come to the assembly of God's
> firstborn children, whose names are
> written in heaven.

> You have come to God himself, the judge
> over all things.

You have come to the spirits of the righteous ones in heaven who have now been made perfect.

You have come to Jesus, the one who mediates the new covenant between God and people, and to the sprinkled blood, which speaks of forgiveness instead of crying out for vengeance.

Can you gaze at this invisible Kingdom, my brother or sister, and know that you are here, belonging to this Kingdom *now?*

Could there be a better place to find ourselves?

Could we be in better company?

Could there be a better covenant between us and the Almighty?

We are now citizens of the Almighty's Kingdom, that complete, unshakable, eternal Kingdom of the Father who has given us this life.

For more words to remind you where you live,
see the appendix for a list of additional Scriptures.

PRAYER TO REJOICE IN THE POWER:

But as for me, I will sing about your power. Each morning I will sing with joy about your unfailing love.

– from PSALM 59:16 –

NEW POWER
FOR LIVING

POWER FOR THOSE WHO BELIEVE

I also pray that you will understand the incredible
greatness of God's power for us who believe him. This is
the same mighty power that raised Christ from the dead.
- from **EPHESIANS 1:19-20** -

One of the saddest moments in the Bible
comes during the trial of Jesus, at the moment
when Peter heard the rooster crowing. Jesus
turned, and their eyes met.

And then Peter remembered. Jesus had told

him this would happen. And Peter certainly remembered, too, how vehemently he had promised that he would always be loyal to Jesus. He would never desert his friend. Peter had declared he would even die for his Lord.

Yet there he was, cursing, and denying that he knew the man on trial.

That's when Jesus turned and looked at His friend.

Can you imagine Peter's shame and his distress, knowing how he had failed?

The account in Luke 22:62 is particularly sad: "And Peter left the courtyard, weeping bitterly."

That lonely and bitter weeping held something we all know—the stinging remorse of failed intentions, regret, and shame.

I can imagine Peter's story, because I have done the same. Every child of God has known the misery of failed intentions and the disappointment when their actions do not live up to what their mouth and heart have promised.

After Jesus had left this earth, we see Peter again, and this time we hear him boldly preaching everywhere and confronting the Jews in the synagogue, and the religious leaders. He's not only confronting, he's also accusing.

"You killed the one who was sent to us by God! You killed the one who could give you life!"

Peter was creating quite an uproar. Oh, yes, it got him into trouble—he was even jailed in an effort to silence him. But when religious leaders threatened him with death if he didn't stop preaching, he refused. "I obey God, not men."

Something had happened to the Peter who had failed his friend so miserably. The Spirit of God had moved in and brought a new power to Peter's life.

Shortly before his death, Peter wrote a letter to believers and assured them of this hope:

> By his divine power, God has given us everything we need for living a godly life.
> (from 2 Peter 1:3)

That's a huge statement to make. We know too well how inadequate we often feel, how overwhelming life can seem. We have shortcomings and weaknesses. We are human, after all! Be honest and stop a moment to reflect on the last week—how many days have you felt that you had everything you needed for living a godly life?

But Peter knew that this is God's truth. He had lived it out. Between the rooster's early-morning crow and the jail cell where Peter spent his last days, something had definitely happened to him.

And God promises that it happens to everyone who believes. As children of God, we've been given an inheritance that includes a power beyond our own resources. And it's available now.

How strong and effective is this power that resides in our lives? How could Peter assert so confidently that Christians have the resources to live as people of God? Take a minute to re-read the Scripture opening this meditation...

The potency and potential of God's power working in us is *incredible.* It's a power so strong that it can raise a dead man—and that power operates in my life now!

This is another instance where we will sound foolish and fanatic to an unbelieving world. But are we going to believe God... or the world?

And so my hope believes God's Word, and goes forward over the bridge of promise; I have a great, supernatural power now available to me for living this life.

It is an incredible promise. But once we stop thinking like the world around us and start believing and living on this hope, then, like Peter, something happens to our lives. Everything changes.

🪶 GOD LIVING IN US 🪶

And this is the secret: Christ lives in you. This gives you
assurance of sharing his glory.

- from COLOSSIANS 1:27 -

Every one of us can have a life changed as dramatically as Peter's. How is it possible?

When we become a son or daughter of the Almighty, a new power moves into our lives—the same power that changed Peter's life.

Listen to one of the last things Jesus said to His disciples, just hours before he died:

> When I am raised to life again, you will know that I am in my Father, and you are in me, and I am in you... All who love me will do what I say. My Father will love them, and we will come and make our home with each of them. (John 14:20, 23)

In my imagination, I can see the disciples grappling with this. Jesus had shocked and angered religious teachers because He claimed to be one with God. That was such a radical claim to make—it was heresy. Now He was saying that He and the Father were going to be "in" the disciples also? How could that happen?

I cannot explain it. How does the Trinity of God Almighty make a home with us? How does Jesus live in us? It can't be logically explained.

But our hope of a new life depends on the promise that God is alive and somehow dwells in those who accept and love Him. *Hope knows this,* even though most of us have not even begun to see the magnitude of what Jesus was saying.

Paul wrote of the mystery of this and of the wonderful results, when he penned the lines about Christ living in us (in the opening verse). In the book of Acts, we hear the early disciples preaching that the Holy Spirit of God was a gift to every believer, Jew or Gentile. The letter to Titus assures us that God generously pours out the Spirit of Christ upon us. In many other places, Scripture says the Spirit of Christ lives in us and the Spirit's power can bring forth amazing things in our lives.

In Jesus' last hours with His disciples, He tells them again and again that the Holy Spirit will be coming to them, that He will be in them. He doesn't want them to miss this. It would be the key to their new lives.

I imagine they were just as puzzled as we are. After all, God living in us? It's a radical claim for us to make, too. But it is what the Word of God says. The Spirit of Christ, the Spirit of God, God, Christ, the Holy Spirit—however you want to name Him—now is alive in us.

This is the key to our new lives... a new power for living.

THE POWER TO CHANGE OUR LIVES

So I say, let the Holy Spirit guide your lives. Then you
won't be doing what your sinful nature craves.
- GALATIANS 5:16 -

I want to live a life devoted to God, but...
There's a problem.

It seems the old me is determined not to die and leave me alone to bask in my new holiness.

We've been given a new life. We belong to Christ's Kingdom. But exactly how do we live this new life we're given as a child of God and a citizen of heaven?

How can I pray for the one at work who treats me so badly?

How can I forgive the wrong that turned my life upside down?

How can I give up the desire to strike back when someone hurts or insults me?

How, in this world, do I love others the way God wants me to love?

How do I break the strength of old desires, the cravings of old weaknesses, the power of old thoughts, and the sting of old wounds?

We all still have those dark parts within us that we know should not be present in the life of a child of God. Scriptures say that our old selfish nature will be with us until the death of our earthly bodies—and the old nature will always be at war with what God wants our lives to show.

So what hope is there of living a new life with that conflict constantly raging, as all of those old things still try to raise their ugly heads and spew their poison?

Hear God's promise:

So now there is no condemnation for those who belong to Christ Jesus. And because you belong to Him, the power of the life-giving Spirit has freed you from the power of sin that leads to death. (Romans 8:1-2)

This is how we live our new lives in Christ's kingdom.

First of all, we live under God's great grace.

We will sometimes fail Him, very much like Peter did, when what we profess and what we do just don't match up. Sin is still part of our humanness. But we are not condemned for our failings.

If we belong to Christ, we are forgiven for the times we fall short of the mark. That is so important to know. It's even more important to take this assurance to heart and live in the freedom it brings.

Secondly, the power of Christ's Spirit living within us can free us from the power of our old nature.

In the western world, society glorifies self-determination, willpower, and strength. Yet we all know those things can quit on us. The "right" attitude can be capricious and undependable. I don't know about you, but I'm sometimes shocked at what rises up out of the dark corners of my heart and mind even when I thought everything was "under control."

But our hope says that we are not at the mercy of our destructive impulses and wrong desires. *We are not*—because we are not living on our own strength. We are in the hands of the Spirit of Christ who lives in us, and His power is greater than anything we can dredge up from our own human resources.

We do have to make the choice, though. We must choose to let the Spirit get to work in our lives.

We must choose to say, "Lord, what I feel toward him is hate. I want revenge, but I know that is not what You want. Holy Spirit, change me, because You know I can't change this myself."

Or, "Father, I never should have said that. It was mean and spiteful and only meant to cut her down a notch or two. She knows exactly how to push all my buttons. Please, please help me hold my tongue."

We must open up the command center of our lives and turn control over to the Spirit of God.

So I say, let the Holy Spirit guide your lives. Then you won't be doing what your sinful nature craves. (Galatians 5:16)

Letting the Spirit control your mind leads to life and peace. (from Romans 8:6)

Both of these are such simple statements. But what great hope those declarations give to those who believe the Father's words to His children!

How does it happen?

That's unexplainable. How can we explain how God works?

But our hope can know that when we set ourselves aside, humble ourselves before God, and say, "I cannot do this. Please lead the way by Your Spirit," our prayers are heard and answered.

When we struggle with things in our lives that we know are not pleasing to God but we think we cannot control or change, this is the answer. This is how our thoughts and actions are changed. This is how we live the life God has called us to live.

This is what brings us life and peace.

ALWAYS WALKING WITH THE TEACHER

If you love me, obey my commandments. And I will ask the
Father, and he will give you another Advocate, who will never
leave you. He is the Holy Spirit, who leads into all truth.

- JOHN 14:15-17 -

As a teacher, the best moments come when I see in the eyes and face of the learner a sudden light that means, "I've got it! I see it now! I know how all the pieces fit!"

During His three years of public teaching, Jesus put forth many new and puzzling thoughts. There had to have been countless times when His disciples struggled to understand and put all the pieces together.

Then, too soon, Jesus told them He was going away.

I can imagine the disappointment the disciples must have felt, as though they were being set adrift. They had left their old, everyday lives behind. They had ridden the ebb and flow of the tide of Jesus' popularity—but now Jesus was leaving and they were left stranded. If I would have been one of the twelve, I would have been devastated.

In the middle of the disciples' grief and confusion about what was happening, during the last evening they were together, Jesus told them at least four times that He was not leaving them stranded; the Holy Spirit was going to come, live in them, and continue teaching and guiding them. This was not the end. He would be coming back to them in a different way.

This is the Spirit that is poured out generously (Titus 3:6) on every child of God—to this very day.

Let's keep this uppermost in our minds as we go about each day: Jesus Christ is alive on this earth. He lives with us. Just as He lived with His disciples in Galilee and taught them every day, He is constantly with us, teaching, reminding, encouraging, and leading to the truth.

When we believe this hope, it changes all of life.

Because we know that now we walk, literally, with Christ—just as surely as Peter, James, and John walked and talked with Him.

And He is continuing our training to be His disciples, teaching us, molding our thinking, showing us truth.

There are countless ways He works every day.

Sometimes, there's a nudge to do something you would never have thought of before or to speak to someone you might have passed by.

Or you've been puzzling over an issue, and a new insight comes.

Or you're given a quiet assurance when you need it.

Or someone else shares what they've learned, and the Spirit says, *Yes, that's right. Pay attention to that.*

Or you read a passage of Scripture and there's a verse that you've never noticed before—and it is exactly what you need for today. It is, literally, God's Word for you at that very moment.

I'm guessing you can add many more examples of how the Spirit teaches you.

The Spirit of Christ is constantly shaping us, helping us along the way, sharpening our sights, giving us those glimpses of the invisible heavenly realm and its realities.

I like to think of Jesus patiently showing me the truth, teaching me the things I need to learn. Every day. Jesus and I aren't by the Sea of Galilee or on the road to Jerusalem. We're taking a walk in the sunshine. We're driving down State Route 39. We're preparing for an interview for a story. We're relaxing by the fire. We're talking with my Bible Read-Thru group or my friends or my sisters or a complete stranger. Oh, yes, and sometimes we do sit on the rocks and gaze at the sea.

Some things take me awhile. But when I finally "get" whatever He's teaching me, in my imagination, I can see the smile of my Teacher.

⮞ BLOOMING! ⮜

For God is working in you, giving you the desire and the
power to do what pleases him.
- **PHILIPPIANS 2:13** -

It was March. My young grandson and I were checking the flowers beds for about the third time that week. We longed to see the first buds of crocuses unfurl their cheerful flags and say, "Ta-da! Here we are! Announcing spring!"

In our corner of the world, winter weather can be quite variable. Some winters are mild—some of my friends have played golf in January. But generally, it's cold, snowy, and icy. In some months there are many cancellations and much sickness. And as much as I love a snowy winter day, the moon glittering on fresh snow, and invigorating, crisp air—by April, the warm sunshine of spring is very welcome.

So the very first crocus that blooms in my flower bed—even when it must poke up through snow—is a cause for celebration.

But, you know what? (And this is obvious, of course.) There is absolutely nothing we can do to melt the snow and bring those crocuses in the flower bed to life. Nothing. We have no power to hasten the unfolding colors.

Isn't that much like the things we long to see blooming in our lives? Love, joy, patience, peace, kindness, a righteous character pleasing to our God—don't we desire to have those burst forth in full bloom in our character and actions?

How successful have you been at forcing those blooms?

I was constantly frustrated. Pretty much failing at the entire checklist. Then, finally, God got through to me with the message of hope in Scriptures like these:

> May you always be filled with the fruit of your salvation—the righteous character produced in your life by Jesus Christ—for this will bring much glory and praise to God. (Philippians 1:11)

> But the Holy Spirit produces this kind of fruit in our lives: love, joy, peace, patience, kindness, goodness, faithfulness, gentleness, and self-control. (from Galatians 5:22-23)

> [Jesus said,] "Yes, I am the vine; you are the branches. Those who remain in me, and I in them, will produce much fruit. For apart from me you can do nothing." (John 15:5)

Do you catch the common idea in these Scriptures? The fruits in our lives that are pleasing to God are produced by the Holy Spirit, our connection to Jesus Christ. We cannot produce these things on our own, no matter how hard we work at it; these things come only from the life of Christ growing in us.

This is a supernatural thing, a mystery. How does the Spirit of God grow a life in us? We cannot explain it, although we can see results.

Don't we take for granted that this same type of thing happens on a smaller, human scale? We say that a boy grows up in the same spirit of his father, or a daughter has the kind spirit of her mother. Children are both born with and learn traits that are patterned after their parents' proclivities. And so it is with us when we have a new life born of the Spirit of God. He instills some of Himself within us and molds and teaches us as we grow in this new life.

I know we don't always feel that God is working in our lives. Sometimes it seems we're caught in the grip of winter, and spring is discouragingly far off. In your tired times, in those moments you feel helpless and hopeless, when you despair because so much in the world seems bigger and more powerful than you, and if the old evils in your spirit keep rising up and threatening to take control, ask the Spirit for assurance of His power working in your life. He will answer that prayer.

This is the great hope that we have: We are in the hands of the Master Gardener. Instead of working at the impossible, frustrating task of *making myself* loving, patient, joyful, and righteous, I turn over control of my thoughts, emotions, and actions to Him and let Him work. Only His power can bring the desired blooms and harvest.

I've found I can't force the blooms of what God wants to grow in my life. But the Holy Spirit, living within, is the One who can bring forth the beauty.

INFINITELY MORE

May [the God of peace] produce in you, through the power of Jesus Christ, every good thing that is pleasing to him.
– from HEBREWS 13:21 –

When we turn over the controls of our lives to Christ's Spirit, we're opening up to a power beyond anything we can imagine. The power of His Spirit can transform us completely. Hope relies on that power as we live out our new life.

I want to draw on His unlimited resources and strength every day.

I want His Spirit to empower me—

- when I feel overwhelmed by circumstances or schedule,

- when I would rather hold on to bitterness than forgive,

- when I am too selfish to live love,

- when people are so annoying that I lose sight of how much God loves them,

- when I'm tempted to think a situation is hopeless,

then I need the power of His resources.

And—hope piled upon hope!—God assures us that His power working in us can accomplish "infinitely more than we ask or think" (Ephesians 3:20).

Once hope knows and relies on this power of God working in us, then we also realize that new lives *are* possible. Then it *is* possible for me to be more kind, for me to treat my enemies differently, for me to forgive. It *is* possible for my character to leave behind its selfishness and begin to produce the things that please God. After all, the power that works in God's children now is the same power that raised a dead man.

Even though Scripture declares that the power of God is so great that what He can do in my life is beyond my imagination, I want to know as much of it as I can!

For more words about the power of the Spirit within us,
see the appendix for a list of additional Scriptures.

**PRAYER AS WE FACE
DEATH AND LIFE:**

My heart is confident in you, O God.

- from PSALM 108:1 -

NEW LIFE
EXPECTANCY

 LIFE THAT LASTS FOREVER

*For you have been born again, but not to a life that will
quickly end. Your new life will last forever because it
comes from the eternal, living word of God.*

― 1 PETER 1:23 ―

It was not a time for pat answers or churchy
clichés. It was a time when I wanted to know
exactly what hope I was depending upon.
My friend had just been given the diagnosis:
lymphoma, a cancer of the blood. She was a very

sick woman, the doctor said, and chemotherapy must begin immediately.

Regardless of what the doctors prescribed, or what they planned and predicted, our thoughts went to our mortality. Our circle of friends is "at that age"—a time when more than gray hair and morning stiffness has begun to assault and break our bodies.

And so we take a hard look at what our hearts truly believe about this life and what happens next. Because, what *does* happen next?

Isn't this a question that we might ask every day? Whether we are in prime physical condition or coping with a body whose end is coming soon, we do not know what tomorrow will bring. We cannot know what curves or detours life will throw into our path.

Even though these thoughts might fit in another book—a volume on our hope for the future—I believe they also belong right here, as we're thinking about how God makes everything new in our lives when we come to Him.

What is new? Our life expectancy.

Those who believe in Jesus Christ now have new, eternal dimensions to this day on earth. The hope of a life that goes on forever shapes our perspective on all of earthly life here and now.

Life goes on after this body wears out. It will

be a life in a different realm, on a different plane. *Forever* and *eternal* are difficult words to grasp; nevertheless, hope knows that a forever, eternal life has already begun in us.

DOING AWAY WITH TIME

I tell you the truth, [Jesus said] those who listen to my message and believe in God who sent me have eternal life. They will never be condemned for their sins, but they have already passed from death into life.

– JOHN 5:24 –

It's a pretty amazing story. King Hezekiah was gravely ill. He was going to die. He knew it, and all those around him knew it. God even sent a prophet to tell Hezekiah to put his affairs in order, because, yes, he was going to die.

But the king pleaded with God to let him live, and the prophet had not even left the palace grounds before God told him to turn around and deliver a new message to Hezekiah: "OK, I'll give you fifteen more years."

"I need a sign, so I can be sure God will do this," said Hezekiah to the prophet.

In answer to the king's request, God made the sundial go crazy—the shadow marking the passing of time moved backwards. Today, we'd look at our clocks and see them going from two o'clock to one o'clock to noon. God turned back time.

Three days later, King Hezekiah had recovered—and he lived fifteen more years, just as God had promised.

When I first read this account, I wondered what it would be like to have absolute assurance from God Himself that He was going to give me exactly fifteen more years to live.

Put yourself in the story—God tells you exactly when you're going to depart this earth. And then, just to be certain that you believe Him, He makes the sun move backwards that day, from west to east! Would you doubt His message? I think I would mark my Day of Departure on my calendar in ink.

Hezekiah's story sounds incredible. But let me tell you—I, too, have received a message from God that He will extend my life.

So have you, if you belong to Christ.

Jesus brought this new message for everyone: Those who belong to Him will live on forever.

The Son of God made it very clear when He said, "Listen to my message and believe it. Then you will not be condemned for your sins and you have eternal life." Jesus Christ holds the key. He holds life.

This is hope: The God who does not lie has

made a firm promise to give His children a life that goes beyond these bodies, beyond earth, beyond years, beyond numbers, and beyond time. And we are already living that life.

When it comes to giving life to His children, God doesn't just scramble time—He does away with time and its limitations. As it turns out, our story and promise are even more fantastic than Hezekiah's.

IMMORTALITY: GOD'S PLAN FOR YOU FROM BEFORE THE BEGINNING

For God saved us and called us to live a holy life. He did this, not because we deserved it, but because that was his plan from before the beginning of time—to show us his grace through Christ Jesus. And now he has made all of this plain to us by the appearing of Christ Jesus, our Savior. He broke the power of death and illuminated the way to life and immortality through the Good News.

– 2 TIMOTHY 1:9-10 –

What word means *before the beginning of time?* Is that an impossible question? We could even say that the title above makes no sense. We think of everything within the framework of beginnings and endings and all that progresses in between.

But eternity does not have those boundaries. How do we go to *before the beginning of time?*

From before the beginning of time, Scripture tells us, God planned for us to live forever.

I have always thought of the "beginning of time" as the time of Adam and Eve's creation. But perhaps, instead, time actually began at the moment their sin brought into the world the curse of death—and thus an ending of this life. Perhaps that is when time began—when we started measuring things with the ending of death.

But we were created to live without such measured limits. We were created in God's image: in immortal dimensions.

We were not created for death or endings!

This is about as far as my mind can go. We can only catch glimpses of the meaning of *eternal* and *immortal.* I see and measure and judge everything by the earthly dimensions of my thinking and with my limited senses, and so immortality is outside my comprehension.

In the last few years, though, I've begun to catch glimpses of the eternal dimensions of the present. The glimpses are fleeting and small; just as I reach out to grasp and savor them, it seems I cannot hold the idea or take it further. Even though the eternal exists now, I imagine that glimpses are all that God can give us at present. We will need new eyes to live fully in the eternal realm.

Trying to imagine or understand a life that does not end can be overwhelming.

What we can grasp, though, is Jesus' message when He appeared on earth to reveal the plan to everyone. "Have faith in Me," He says. "Through Me, you will have the immortality that God created you to have."

Before the beginning, God planned for us to be immortal! I find great comfort in knowing God has a plan for me outside of and beyond these short breaths on earth.

Ask the Father to give you a glimpse—just a glimpse!—of His plans for your immortality.

BREAKING THE SLAVERY TO FEAR

*Because God's children are human beings—made of flesh
and blood—the Son also became flesh and blood. For only
as a human being could he die, and only by dying could he
break the power of the devil, who had the power of death.
Only in this way could he set free all who have lived their
lives as slaves to the fear of dying.*

– **HEBREWS 2:14-15** –

The shadow of death hangs over every one of us. Every day takes each of us closer to the moment our earthly life will end. We can try to ignore it, but we can never avoid it. Our bodies, in their flesh-and-blood existence, grow old and die. We fear what lies ahead for ourselves, and we fear the loss of others dear to us.

We've all felt the clutches of this fear. Death sends great tremors through our thoughts and hearts.

Christ lived on earth under the same cloud; He was flesh and blood, and He would die. There was no avoiding it.

And when we read of His agonizing in Gethsemane, we know that facing death and accepting that this was the Father's will was no easy thing for Jesus. He was the Son of God, who would soon be given supreme power over everything on earth and in heaven—yet that night, He suffered as any human who is facing death.

This makes His resurrection an even greater triumph. When Christ—in His body—came out of the grave and again walked among His friends on earth, God was announcing to the world that He was taking another step in His plan to make all things new. A flesh-and-blood human being had died, but God's power had beaten death!

Who of us can say we have a plan or the power to beat death?

Every child of God!

The death that rules in this world has no power over those who belong to the Resurrected One. They belong to Him; and the promise they have is that they'll share in the same resurrection.

And so, this also is a new thing in our new lives: Christ breaks the slavery to the fear of dying.

I examine my own life. In what ways does the fear of dying still control me? Christ went through suffering and death to set me free from that fear. How can shedding this fear change my life? What freedom will that bring?

Hope knows that this short and troubled life is not "all there is." Death is not the end of us. God invaded death's territory and beat it. And He has planned an even greater future for those He has invited to become His children.

~~~ CONFIDENCE OF OUR IMMORTALITY ~~~

This truth gives them confidence that they have eternal
life, which God—who does not lie—promised
them before the world began.

– TITUS 1:2 –

It is one thing to read that God promises eternal life and to intellectually assent to believing this. But our capacity to grasp *eternal* is so limited. What about our times of doubt? What if we aren't so confident of God's promise of immortality for His children? What if that truth hasn't yet sunk into our bones (figuratively speaking) so that we are certain of this hope?

Ah, yet again, our Shepherd God provides in His Word exactly what we need.

The Scripture above opens a letter from the apostle Paul to a pastor of new churches. Before he closes that letter, he repeats this assurance one more time: God, in His grace, will give us what we need to build our confidence in our immortality. I'm sure that in the time of the early church, just as today, there were questions and doubts. We humans have such limited sight!

But God bolsters our confidence *by His truth,* found in the Word and in Jesus Christ, and made plain to us by the Holy Spirit.

His truth. God's Word teaches us how to live

in His paths—in His eternity, if you will—even while we are living within our earthly dimensions.

His Son. Jesus says that all of God's truth resides in Him. Knowing Jesus, learning from Him, trusting Him with our lives, and putting ourselves in His hands and in His service—this puts us smack dab where we need to be to have our understanding illuminated by God's truth.

His Spirit. And then there's that amazing promise—God puts His Spirit within each of His children, a connection that tunes us into God's thinking; even, Paul says, to the "secrets" of God! (Remember 1 Corinthians 2:10-12)

God knows we have trouble seeing beyond this earthly world. He doesn't leave us floundering around, trying on our own effort to believe huge promises we can barely grasp. And so He has given us these things to help us be certain of our hope.

The more we get to know Jesus and the more we seek His truth, the more His Spirit will work to give us the sight to see eternal things and grow our confidence of our life in the eternal realm.

 THE FREE GIFT

Because of [God's] grace he declared us righteous and gave
us confidence that we will inherit eternal life.

- TITUS 3:7 -

Sometimes I lose sight of what an amazing gift I've been given. But let me tell you, if you want a fervent appreciation of God's grace and His gift of life to all of us, then spend a week reading the Old Testament prophets like Jeremiah.

In the words of those prophets, we hear God's blistering condemnation of His own chosen people. They had decided they did not need Him and had given their lives to all kinds of other idolatrous pursuits and passions—and God was not happy with the state of things. (This is putting it mildly.)

You'll read things in Jeremiah that you never thought you'd hear a loving God say—things like "I'm going to abandon you. I'm tired of constantly giving you another chance. You are nothing to me now. Every wonderful thing I had for you, I'm going to tear away from you. I'm going to look the other way while your enemies slaughter you. Yes, I've even brought your enemies here to do just that. Your corpses will be picked clean by the wild animals." Oh, His language was much stronger and terrifying. His judgment was coming, and it was going to be awful.

As God brought His case against Israel and Judah, I can see myself in some of His words describing the people with whom He's so angry. I see our country there, too. Many of the words in Jeremiah especially could have been written about the United States today. I cringe as I read.

What's my point?

Reading Jeremiah reminded me again what a great gift I've been given—the gift of a forever life and a cleansed, unhindered relationship with our Creator God. I could never be spotless and blameless in His eyes—at least, not on my own. Things would be pretty hopeless without Jesus Christ and what He did for me.

> So just as sin ruled over all people and brought them to death, now God's wonderful grace rules instead, giving us right standing with God and resulting in eternal life through Jesus Christ our Lord. (Romans 5:21)

> For the wages of sin is death, but the free gift of God is eternal life through Christ Jesus our Lord. (Romans 6:23)

This eternal life is what we were meant to have at the beginning, when God created us in His own image. But the human race lost the life God had planned for them when they decided they wanted to do things their own way instead of according to God's plan.

Yet the Creator loves His creation and woos it back. He became one of us, lived a life none of us would ever choose, and died an agonizing death as a human—all so that He could offer us this gift.

The gift is life, the life and the relationship with Him that we once lost.

Without Jesus, I'd be headed for the terrifying disaster that was about to fall on Jeremiah's people.

Instead, I'm enjoying this free gift.

And what can I say except, *Father, thank you?*

It's nothing I've done or could do. The gift comes from His kindness and mercy.

The Bible app on my phone has a "Verse of the Day" feature. And I'm telling you, sometimes I am positive that God rearranges the schedule of verses just for me, because He knows the words I need to hear from Him that day.

I had spent a week reading Jeremiah, all those blistering bulletins of God's wrath and judgment about to fall on the Israelites (and other nations, too). That's when I first wrote the previous thoughts about being so, so grateful for God's grace and Jesus' rescuing me so that I can live without terror of judgment and as a beloved child of God. That same day, I was refreshed yet again when I took a look at the Bible app's Verse of the Day:

> No power in the sky above or in the earth below—indeed, nothing in all creation will ever be able to separate us from the love of God that is revealed in Christ Jesus our Lord. (Romans 8:39)

Familiar lines, but so reassuring to my hope.

Instead of hearing this message: "No power in heaven or earth can keep my punishment from falling on you,"

We now hear: "Come back to me. My love has cleared the way. Nothing in heaven or earth can put you outside my love."

THE CHOICE THAT IS THE KEY TO LIFE

"God loved the world so much that he gave his one and only Son, so that everyone who believes in him will not perish but have eternal life."
- JOHN 3:16, JESUS SPEAKING -

There's no opting out. Each one of us must make a choice.

This choice is essentially the same one that

Moses presented to the Israelites:

> Today I have given you the choice between life and death, between blessings and curses... Oh, that you would choose life, so that you and your descendants might live! You can make this choice by loving the LORD your God, obeying him, and committing yourself firmly to him. This is the key to your life. (from Deuteronomy 30:19-20)

That was the way Moses laid out the choice for the people of Israel. He reminded them of the covenant the Lord had made with them and everything God had already done for them. This is the key to life, he said. Stick to this covenant God has made with us.

Jeremiah also relayed words of the Lord, describing this choice as standing at a crossroads. "Look around," God says, "and find the way of this covenant with Me. Travel that path, and you'll find rest for your souls" (from Jeremiah 6:16).

Doesn't that result sound enticing? *You'll find rest for your souls.*

The crossroads for us is where we meet Jesus. We don't have to look too hard for the right way—Jesus stands there and says plainly that HE is the way. HE is the one who can give life.

A crossroads demands a choice. God made a covenant with us; Jesus sealed it with His blood. God will never revoke or cancel it. Are we going to choose the path of this covenant? Or are we going to reject it?

Hope knows that this is still the key to life—for us right here, right now, and in the forever. Love the Lord, obey Him, and commit firmly to Him.

For more truths to make us confident,
see the appendix for a list of additional Scriptures.

PRAYER AS WE LIVE OUT
NEW IDENTITY:

Teach me how to live, O Lord.
Lead me along the right path.

– **from PSALM 27:11** –

NEW IDENTITY
AND PURPOSE

 INVITED TO BE HIS PEOPLE

Once you had no identity as a people;
now you are God's people.
- **from 1 PETER 2:10** -

Have you ever stood on a diving board and looked down into the deep end of the pool, knowing that your swimming ability is alarmingly inadequate?

That's where I'm standing now. As though I'm getting ready to jump into the deep end, but I know I'm going to have to paddle and kick like crazy to get through this.

Just to review, we've been focusing on how God makes all things new when we come to Him: We have a new friendship with God, new access to Him, a new status and a new heart, a new life in a new realm, and a new power for living with a new life expectancy.

There's another new thing that transforms our lives: We're also given a new identity and purpose.

This is why I'm taking a deep breath as I contemplate diving in here. We could write an entire book about this, not just one chapter. There is so much in Scripture that tells us who we are now and what our purpose is in this life, right where we are, right now, today. These short meditations can only give glimpses of all this truth.

So here we go. I guess we'll just jump right in.

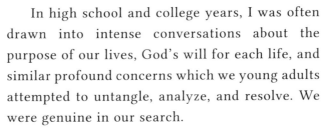

In high school and college years, I was often drawn into intense conversations about the purpose of our lives, God's will for each life, and similar profound concerns which we young adults attempted to untangle, analyze, and resolve. We were genuine in our search.

But life gets busy. Marriage, children, jobs,

bills, church, social commitments... The weeks slip away into years, and we often don't give much thought to the purpose of our lives. We're too busy dealing with what's right in front of us to think about finding answers to nebulous questions.

Until one day we suddenly see that we've been floating along—well, maybe racing along— and half our life (or more) is gone. And something gives us pause and we wonder again, *Why am I here? Is there a purpose to my life?*

We frequently hear versions of these sentiments:

"I just don't know who I am."

"What's the point?"

"Why am I here?"

"I'd love to know God's purpose for my life, but how do I know what it is?"

God has some very tender words for His children:

"You have been chosen to know me, believe in me, and understand that I alone am God. There is no other God—there never has been, and there never will be."

That's from Isaiah 43:10. At that point, God was addressing Israel, a people whom God had chosen to have a special relationship with Him. Listen to other phrases the Scriptures use in reference to God's people:

- "My own special treasure."
- "My very own people and special possession."
- A holy people who belong to the Lord God.
- Chosen as the objects of His love.
- "Made for myself and for my glory."

God had a distinctive, intentional relationship with the Israelite nation, even during the times they turned their backs on Him. Then, on the road to Damascus, the story took a huge turn when the resurrected Jesus appeared to Saul and said, "I'm going to send you to the Gentiles, so they, too, will turn to God and will become part of God's people."

In other words, Jesus opened the door and issued an invitation to everyone to enjoy this special relationship with God. Now we also are His special treasure, belonging to Him; His masterpiece, His very own people. We're chosen to know Him in a special way, "called to belong to Jesus," as Paul puts it (Romans 1:6).

Called? What does that mean?

The Word Study System of my NLT Bible tells me that the Greek words used in the New Testament that we have translated as *called* or *calling* mean *an invitation to someone to accept responsibilities for a particular task or a new relationship. God calls/invites the believer to relationship with him or to a particular role in his Kingdom.*

We are invited to believe in Jesus and His message. If we do, we become a part of God's people. Citizens of heaven. Children of the Almighty God. Treasured. Loved. Chosen to have a special relationship with Him. Heirs to all the promises He has made.

If you are married, how did your life change the day of your wedding? If you are a parent, what happened to your thinking when your child was born? If you are a manager in your workplace, did anything change when you were promoted to that position? If you are a caretaker of an elderly parent or an ill spouse, how has that altered your life?

The point is, when we find ourselves with a new identity, our lives take on a new shape. Our thinking, our actions, our emotions, our heart, the way we spend our money, even our schedules—every part of us is affected. We are changed because this new identity has brought new purpose to our lives.

As we shall see, our new identity as God's people also brings us a new and definite purpose.

～ BEING GOD'S HOLY PEOPLE ～

I am writing... to you who have been called by God to be
his own holy people.
- from 1 CORINTHIANS 1:2 -

Imagine receiving a good, old-fashioned letter in the mail. Remember those? Okay, if it works better for you to imagine an email or text, put yourself in that picture.

You see the return address, and you know immediately that it's from your pastor.

You wonder what this could be about, and you tear open the envelope (or click the email) and scan through the first lines.

Dear You, (the note reads) *I am writing to those of you whom God has called to be His holy people....*

What's this?

Would your first reaction be a thought that the letter had probably been addressed to you by mistake?

Did you know that God has called you to be one of His holy people?

Are you ready for that assignment?

Are you qualified to be chosen to take a place among the holy people of God?

Do you even want to be holy?

The apostle Paul began his letter to the new Christian church in Corinth with the same words used in your pastor's letter to you. Now, if you go on to read the remainder of the Corinthian letters, you'll know that this church had just as many problems as we have in our churches today, including divided loyalties to leaders, invasive cultural influences, and serious sexual sins. I mean, come on. How could Paul possibly think these people could ever be among the holy people of God?

Because God says so.

He says all those who belong to Jesus Christ are invited to be His holy people.

Somewhere in our history, our English language has attached undesirable connotations to the word *holy*. Do we react to that word in a negative way because we know how far we are from the standard of *holy?* Is it the deep and stubborn perversity of our sin nature that rebels against this word we connect most closely to God? Is it because a human distortion of God's truth has made *holy* an impossible thing in our minds?

Whatever the reason, let's ask the Spirit to erase all our previous emotional reactions to this word and let's take a fresh look at being God's holy people.

My concordance gives three ways in which

the word *holy* can be used, and Scripture applies all of these definitions to each child of God.

"Consecrated or set aside for sacred use." When God first chose Israel and called them His holy nation, He outlined His plans for them. They would be a light to other nations, a blessing among the peoples of the world. In our own time, God's holy nation includes everyone belonging to Jesus Christ. We, too, are to be dedicated to showing God's goodness and compassion to the world. We are the channel He uses to spread His love and forgiveness and mercy to the world that doesn't yet know Him. God has sacred purposes for us in this world.

"Standing apart from sin and evil." Yes, our God hates sin. It is the enemy's corruption of God's good creation. Yes, God desires that His children grow up into His way of living—which is the path of true life. We still struggle with sin. Being God's holy people does not mean our lives are flawless. Christ gave us a "perfect" standing in God's eyes, but we're still learning how to live. Hebrews 12:10 says that God disciplines us so that we can share in His holiness. Our Father is teaching us, forming our character for this new life we've been given.

We strive to stand apart from sin for another reason—we live according to God's laws so that we can be a light shining on the hill in Satan's dark world. God's holy people are here to show that there is a better way.

"Characteristic of God." God's children are also to grow up into His character! Ephesians 4:24 assures us that the new nature we were given at our second birth was created to be like God—"truly righteous and holy." (Pause right now and think about this: You were given a new nature that was created to be like God!) And so we are learning to be like our Father, learning to show His compassion, love, mercy, justice, and purity. Again, it is through us that God shows the world who He is and what He does. Isn't it amazing that He wants us to be a part of the execution of His plan?

Back to that letter addressed to those invited to be God's holy people.

Being holy is *not* about being flawless and perfect. It's about a dedicated relationship—about whose you are and who you serve.

We are living in Satan's domain. Of course, Satan and his world want to lie about and mock the significance of being *holy.* Don't let his tactics deter you.

Instead, shed all those lies and ponder what a

wonder and privilege it is to be invited to be part of God's holy people.

HIS KINGDOM OF PRIESTS

You are royal priests, a holy nation, God's very own possession. As a result, you can show others the goodness of God, for he called you out of the darkness into his wonderful light.

– 1 PETER 2:9 –

Here's an additional book I'd like to write—thoughts on what God is telling us when He gives us another new name: *my kingdom of priests, my royal priests,* and *a holy nation of priests.*

To be honest, up until a few years ago, these phrases meant nothing to me. I grew up in the Mennonite church, and priests and their duties were not a part of my experience. Even though these references appear again and again in the Christian letters of the New Testament, whatever God was saying about us being priests was totally lost on me.

Paul and Peter and the other writers of the New Testament, however, knew exactly what it meant to be a priest. Priests were a part of the

Jewish culture since the days of Abraham (maybe even before that). The New Testament writers understood all that the name *priest* implied.

Then, a few years ago, I began participating in an annual Bible Read-Thru group, and I started to pay more attention to the priests in Jewish history and tradition and make note of their responsibilities and purpose.

Because I'm still pondering what it means for me to be part of God's royal priesthood, let me simply share some of the Old Testament references that have given me food for thought.

- The Lord said the priesthood was a "special privilege of service" (Numbers 18:7). It seems that our Lord, by calling us His royal priests, is giving us a special privilege of service to Him.

- The priests carried the Ark of the Covenant. This box contained the tablets of God's law and was the place where God was considered to be physically present. Priests stood before God as His ministers, and they pronounced blessings in His name (Deuteronomy 10:8). Today, the people of God "carry" His presence in this world. We're entrusted with Christ's Gospel. Pronouncing blessings in

His name? Yes, we're to do that in this world—even to our enemies and those who mistreat us. But what does it mean to stand before God as His ministers? I don't know that yet... I welcome your insights.

- The priests were to lead the people in worship, to invoke God's blessings, to give thanks and praise the Lord (1 Chronicles 16:4). Most certainly, the children of God in today's world should be praying and worshiping and praising.

- Solomon's prayer of dedication for the new Temple included this line: "May your priests be clothed in godliness" (2 Chronicles 6:41). Aha. Here we are back to that idea of godliness. Our lives are to be wrapped up and defined by our special relationship to God.

- Everywhere in the Old Testament, we see the priests as the ones who offered up sacrifices to the Almighty. Yes, we offer sacrifices too. We can't *earn* God's love, but we can respond to His love with our worship and offerings.

What kind of offerings do we bring? They're not slaughtered animals or birds or pure oils or the choicest grain. The Scriptures tell us that our offerings are:

- a broken, repentant heart (Psalm 51:16-17)

- showing love and seeking to know the Lord (Hosea 6:6)

- thankfulness (Psalm 50:14)

- doing what is good, loving mercy, walking humbly before God (Micah 6:8 and Hebrews 13:16)

- continual praise (Hebrews 13:15)

- proclaiming our allegiance to Him (Hebrews 13:15)

- sharing with those in need (Hebrews 13:16 and Philippians 4:18)

- giving our bodies—every part of who we are—to God for his service (Romans 12:1)

And here's the amazing thing—our sacrifices are pleasing to God. Peter writes that we are God's holy priests and "through the mediation of Jesus Christ, you offer spiritual sacrifices that please God."

Do you get the power of that picture? We have come from being God's enemies to being priests of this holy, holy God, and what we offer Him through our worship and daily living are offerings acceptable and pleasing to Him—all because Christ has made good our standing with the Almighty.

In the Old Testament, the tribe of Levi was designated to carry on the priestly duties. If one was born a Levite, his career path was set from the moment he was born. Is our career path set the moment we're born into God's family? Yes. I think so.

God tells us what the relationship was meant to be between Him and his priests. It's revealing. Read it carefully. I think it also speaks about God's relationship to and plans for His nation of priests today:

> The purpose of my covenant with the Levites was to bring life and peace, and that is what I gave them.
>
> This required reverence from them, and they greatly revered me and stood in awe of my name.
>
> They passed on to the people the truth of the instructions they received from me. They did not lie or cheat; they walked with me, living good and righteous lives, and they turned many from lives of sin.
>
> The words of a priest's lips should preserve knowledge of God, and people should go to him for instruction, for the priest is the messenger of the LORD of Heaven's Armies. (Malachi 2:5-7)

Bringing life and peace. Living with reverence and awe of the Lord. Teaching truth. Right living. Bringing lives out of sin. Preserving knowledge of God. A messenger of God.

This royal priesthood is indeed a special privilege of service. We were slaves in the dark kingdom. Now we have been set free and adopted as children of God. And not only that—He has made us His priests, sharing His work here on earth, a people through whom He accomplishes His purposes.

UNQUALIFIED AND INADEQUATE

And this is the secret: Christ lives in you.
- from COLOSSIANS 1:27 -

Did the previous pages make you feel tired and burdened?

After reading all of that about our new identity and purpose in life, are you overwhelmed, thinking, *That's way beyond me. How could I ever do and be all that?*

When Jesus was gathering His disciples, He did not seem to place a high priority on qualifications for the assignment He would give them. At least, not the qualifications we might expect. He was going to leave His work to these men—the task of bringing the world back to the Creator. He would turn over this mission to His chosen circle.

But who did He choose? Small-town, average Joes. Some were uneducated. We know that at least one was a social outcast, despised by his neighbors. We don't know all of the disciples well, but in those we do know, we see personality traits that might cause us to scrap their applications if we were choosing people to work in Christ's ministry. Among the disciples there were hot tempers, doubting minds, greedy spirits, critical and judgmental attitudes, mouths too quick to speak, and minds often too slow to grasp what Jesus was trying to teach them.

Oh yes, Jesus' hand-picked, close associates were just like us.

Yet what they did after Jesus left the earth would change the world.

The secret is in this new power for living we've been given. I need to remind myself, often, that drawing on this power of God is the only way I can fulfill this new purpose God has given me. The *only* way.

Two letters make all the difference: IN.

After Jesus' resurrection, there was a huge

shift in God's relationship to men and women. And it's all in the preposition. (Yes, the grammar teacher in me has now emerged.)

Before Christ came to earth, coming *into* God's presence was a completely different thing. One had to come with the proper sacrifice, proper prayers, and proper attitude. One came to the proper place, and priests had to be properly dressed, right down to their underwear. I imagine it all as coming into a throne room, coming only at special times, with special permission and procedures, hoping the great King will give you an audience.

But ever since Christ's resurrection and ascension to heaven, the preposition has been *in*. Now—incredibly—God dwells *in* His people, in a relationship more intimate than we have with even our closest family.

Take a look at Scriptures, and notice those two little letters:

Remain in me, and I will remain in you. (John 15:4)

Christ will make his home in your hearts. (Ephesians 3:17)

Christ lives in me. (Galatians 2:20)

God has made the light of His glory shine in our hearts. (2 Corinthians 4:6)

Righteous character will be produced in you by Christ Jesus. (Philippians 1:11)

This is the secret, really, of our new lives. Everything flows from Christ's life and character *in* us—being a holy people, being priests of the Lord Almighty, fulfilling the rest of the mission (which we'll look at further in the next pages). All of it is possible not because of who or what we are, but because God now lives in His children on earth.

That sounds radical. It is. It was radical in Jesus' day, too, when He said He and the Father were in each other.

John's Gospel begins with Jesus coming into the world "as the true light." Jesus called Himself the light of the world. Then, in His teaching, He also tells His disciples that *they/we* are the light of the world!

How can we be? We are no more qualified for this job than were the first disciples.

This is what hope knows: It is not our light that shines—it is His, shining in us. And He is the one who places the lights exactly where He wants His light to shine in the dark world.

It is His light shining in us that the apostle Paul compares to a great treasure contained in fragile clay jars. "This makes it clear that our great power is from God, not from ourselves" (2 Corinthians 4:7).

God said His power actually works best in our weakness (2 Corinthians 12:9). When it is clear that we are unqualified and inadequate for the mission, it will be obvious that is only God's power at work in our lives—not our own skills and strength. The light in us, the strength in us, the compassion, the love, the mercy—all of that is nothing we could do on our own.

Only God can do these things. We are to stand as testimony that what people see in our lives is possible only because God exists and His power works in us. There is only one explanation for my new life: God.

Jesus was a flesh-and-blood-like-us embodiment of God in this world. And we're to be the same. We are humans, walking on this earth, with God in us and working through us.

God's children are here for a reason—the same reason Christ came to the earth—to show the world who God is and bring men and women back to their Creator.

But I'm not a woman who would or could do that on my own. Not me. I'm unqualified and inadequate.

Only God in me will do it.

 TEMPLE OF HOPE

*Don't you realize that all of you together are the temple of
God and that the Spirit of God lives in you?*
- 1 CORINTHIANS 3:16 -

Soon after God rescued His people from exile
and slavery in Egypt, they were given a physical,
tangible reminder of His presence with them. For
a period of time, a portable, tent-like structure
was seen as God's "dwelling place." Eventually,
under King Solomon's supervision, a grand and
lavish Temple was built.

To the Jewish people, the Temple was

- filled with God's presence

- where one came to acknowledge God

- where mercy and forgiveness were found

- where one came to to put their life to rights

Invaders from Babylon destroyed Solomon's
Temple, and much later another was built. That
structure, too, was destroyed (this time, by the
Romans) about seventy years after the birth of
Christ.

But while that second Temple still stood,
the apostle Peter wrote to God's chosen people
scattered all over the world, and described a new
Temple, a new place God was building where He
had chosen to reside:

And you are living stones that God is building into his spiritual temple. (from 1 Peter 2:5)

Up until the time Peter was writing, God's people had looked to the physical structure of the Temple as the sign of and the place of God's presence in their world. Now, Peter says, God is doing a new thing. God is building a spiritual Temple for Himself—and you are the stones He is using to build!

Even though Solomon's Temple was incredibly lavish, the wise king acknowledged that no one could possibly build a home fit for the Lord. Now God Himself is building the home He desires here on earth—and He is building it with the raw material of His invited and holy people.

Everything in the physical Temples pointed to God and was carefully designed to mend the relationship between individuals and God and to bring people back into the reverence and presence of their Creator.

God's children, rescued from the kingdom of darkness and slavery, now become the home where He chooses to live.

He takes us, living stones, and builds something tangible—a "temple," evidence that He is in this world and that His presence makes a difference.

And this spiritual Temple is to stand in the world, announcing the message of hope, pointing people back to reverence and relationship with the Creator.

This makes a difference in how I tackle whatever lies ahead today. In how I treat others. In how I work with others in the church. In how I respond to forces in the world around me and to events that happen to me.

I have a new perspective on wherever I find myself today. Now I stand as one of the stones in the Temple of God, a place of His presence on this earth.

He is building a place where *He is*. We are that temple from which God declares to the world, "I am here. Come back to me and I'll give you hope."

ENTRUSTED WITH THE MISSION

Urging you to defend the faith that God has entrusted once for all time to his holy people.
- from JUDE 1:3 -

The events we commemorate each Easter weekend mark a turning point in the history of the world, the beginning of a new era in the relationship between God and humanity.

The overall story is huge: God created the world for Himself, but it decided to go another way. Still loving us, throughout all the history of humanity God has called us back to Him.

With the crucifixion of Jesus, God was doing a completely new thing. He Himself was giving and being the sacrifice that paid the price to buy back His beloved creation.

This creation is enslaved to the enemy. We were born into this slavery to sin and rebellion against God. God did not buy us to make us His slaves—He bought us to free us, adopt us, bring us into His family, and make us heirs to everything in His Kingdom!

So Christ's resurrection signaled a new direction and hope for everyone: Death to the old life, resurrection to new life!

Yet this new life does not remove us from this world. Here we are now, children of God, living in this world that is ruled by the powers of sin. And while we are still here, Christ says to all His disciples, "Just as the Father sent me into this world, so I'm sending you."

Christ came with this message: *There is one God who rules, and there is peace with Him, if you will only believe it and accept it. And when you make peace with God, there is also a new life for you.*

When Christ's work on earth was finished and He left, He handed the message to all those who follow Him in all times of history, and said, "Deliver this. I'm sending you into the world with this message, just as God sent me."

Want new purpose for your life, child of God? Jesus Christ has entrusted us with the message and asked that we continue His mission in this world.

THE FUTURE OF THE MISSION

The LORD's good plan will prosper in his hands.
— from ISAIAH 53:10 —

We know well that oft-repeated verse called the "Great Commission," but we sometimes miss Jesus' words just before: "I have been given all authority in heaven and on earth" (Matthew 28:18).

The one we follow now has the ultimate authority over everything in heaven and earth.

We are not merely His followers. Now we are His partners, sharing His mission as we are sent into the world as God's ambassadors, trusted messengers, priests, and dwelling place of God's presence.

Here's a line of prophecy to ponder. Isaiah 53 is a passage about Christ's suffering on the cross in order to make us righteous and whole. Verse 10 sets forth seeming contrasts: God's *good* plan was to *crush* Jesus. He died young, as a pauper and criminal. *Yet* He will have many descendants and enjoy a long life,

> ... and the LORD's good plan will prosper in his hands. (v.10)

For all of us called to be in partnership with Christ, these are reassuring words. This prophecy tells us exactly where this road is taking us: God's plan is rolling onwards, there is so much more beyond physical death, and the mission is in good hands!

Not our hands, remember, but Christ's, who lives in us to continue His work in making God known to the world who has ignored and rejected Him.

This is why we don't give up. Why we continue to follow Christ in whatever He gives us to do. The future of the mission is bright.

This takes us down the road to the future—a road where God has given us countless bridges of promise to keep our hope moving forward. It's the subject of another book, but the seeds of the future are right now, in the new identity and purpose we have been given as the holy people of God.

For more truths about our new identity and purpose, see the appendix for a list of additional Scriptures.

PRAYER FOR THE HEIRS OF GOD:

You have given me an inheritance reserved for those who fear you.

– **from PSALM 61:5** –

NEW
INHERITANCE

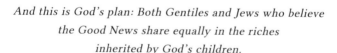 **A NEW INHERITANCE**

And this is God's plan: Both Gentiles and Jews who believe
the Good News share equally in the riches
inherited by God's children.

– from EPHESIANS 3:6 –

On Wednesday mornings as I walk early,
green garbage cans line our street. And the
question often tugs at me: What if I was walking
this street for the sole purpose of finding breakfast
in that garbage? What if I did not have my cozy
nest to return to after my walk? Where would

I go? What if my only option to stay warm at night was to sleep in the recycling bins behind the antique store?

Spiritually, I did live like that. Too long. Sometimes, I still find myself in those old habits and have to remind myself: *No longer! You have a different life now!*

My initial search for the hope that Christians have was triggered by a piece written by George MacDonald, a Scottish preacher and storywriter of the 1800s. He wrote from the struggles of poverty and his battles with depression.

In *Diary of an Old Soul*, MacDonald described a child in the streets, ragged, dirty, scrounging in the gutters for food, fighting to survive. Unknown to the child, he is an heir of the king. The king sits on his throne, wondering where his child is, how he is faring... and waiting, waiting to give his child all of the riches of his kingdom. If only the child would come to him! All the child needs to do is run to the palace and claim his inheritance, and life in the streets would be over.

I could not forget that image and the thought that I often feel exactly like that child—scrounging for sustenance, barely staying alive, ragged and dirty. That was not the life for a child of the King!

Scripture is liberally seasoned with references to the inheritance given to all children of God, to the riches and treasures for those who belong to Christ. A Christian for decades, I nevertheless had no idea what those phrases really meant. Not an inkling.

If you received notice that you have an inheritance waiting to be claimed, wouldn't you want to know what it is? Wouldn't you be eager to claim it and make it yours?

Paul wrote that he was given the privilege of telling everyone about the endless treasures available to them through Christ (Ephesians 3:8). Well, I wanted to know what my endless treasures were.

Yes, I was a starving child on the streets. And I was tired of just scraping by.

CHANGING OUR THINKING

Now you are no longer a slave but God's own child. And since you are his child, God has made you his heir.
- GALATIANS 4:7 -

I don't want to mislead you. If you are reading onward, hoping for an outline of exactly what your new inheritance is, you won't find it in these pages—at least, not in this book. That's part of another book in the Hope Knows series, a book in which we ponder how we can get through each day because of the "rich treasures" God supplies for our use. But for now, we simply want to change how we think and how we see ourselves.

Take a moment to re-read God's word to us in the opening verse...

For a long time, I did see myself as a slave. I thought a relationship with God was based on a long list of *Thou shalts* and *Thou shalt nots,* and I was expected to follow that list as closely as possible... or else!

But Jesus Christ changed all that. Now we have a new relationship with our Creator. Putting our lives in Christ's hands makes us children of God, not slaves to His will but heirs of all He has for His people, both now and in the future (Galatians 3:26).

Do you know anyone who is blessed in abundance with wealth, blessings of family, or an excellent job—yet they seem miserable? They are blind to the wonderful things they've been given, and so they never appreciate and enjoy those things. And you just want to say to them, "Wake up! Be thankful! Look at what you have!"

I don't want to be in that spiritual condition, blind to what I've been given, unable to enjoy the "endless treasures" He has given me, just plodding along and missing the life I could have.

We're told in 1 Corinthians 2:12 that one of the reasons God's Spirit lives in us is to share God's thoughts with us, "so we can know the wonderful things God has freely given us."

I want to know.

So I pray the Spirit of God will open our eyes to who we really are in His plan... and what He has for His children.

That's all, Father... Just open our eyes.

TRUE CHILDREN, TRUE HEIRS

The LORD has promised wonderful blessings for Israel!
- from NUMBERS 10:29 -

Listening to the audio of Mark Twain's "The Prince and the Pauper" with my grandson, I was struck by the spiritual parallels.

In Twain's story, two boys switch places in life. The prince suffers the hardship of the pauper's life, and the boy who grew up in poverty suddenly finds himself surrounded with luxury he had never imagined and wields great power with the utterance of only a word or two.

We're like that destitute boy who miraculously finds himself in the life of a prince—we've been given a life of new and unimagined privilege.

In Numbers 10:29, the Israelites are on the move through the wilderness, leaving Mt. Sinai where God had given them His commandments and traveling toward the Promised Land. Moses had married a Midianite woman, and now he invites his brother-in-law to come with them.

> We are on our way to the place the LORD promised us, for He said, 'I will give it to you.' Come with us and we will treat you well, for the LORD has promised wonderful blessings for Israel!

The Israelites were a people God had chosen for a special relationship with Him, special protection, and special blessings. But in this simple exchange, someone outside the physical lineage of Abraham is given an invitation to share in those blessings. "Come with us; God has promised wonderful blessings for His people."

Today, this invitation is given to everyone.

> For you are all children of God through faith in Christ Jesus. And now that you belong to Christ, you are the true children of Abraham. You are his heirs, and God's promise to Abraham belongs to you. (Galatians 3:26, 29)

Keep this in mind when you read Scripture

about "Israel" or "children of Abraham." No matter your race, ancestry, or church affiliation, your faith in Christ Jesus has made you heirs to all the promises God has made to His children in all times.

Everything God has planned for His people—blessings today, amazing wonders in the future—is now ours. Colossians tells us we have reason for great joy and gratitude because God "has enabled you to share in the inheritance that belongs to his people, who live in the light" (Colossians 1:12).

In God's plan, He has wonderful blessings for His people. And He's given us the invitation to be a part of what He has planned.

PLACE OF PRIVILEGE

Because of our faith, Christ brought us into this place of undeserved privilege where we now stand.
– from ROMANS 5:2 –

Most of us live in relative obscurity. A few of you out there might be famous, but most of us lead very ordinary lives. We're loved and important to a small circle, but that's the extent of our renown and distinction.

So when the Creator and Lord of the universe tells us we are now in a really good place (in today's lingo), do we hear Him?

My first reaction to the opening verse above is that I tend to focus on that other word—*undeserved.* Yes, everything God has given me is undeserved. We of Mennonite and Amish background especially are taught the importance of humility, and I suppose that's Biblical, but... We already know how undeserving we are—until Jesus solved that problem for us. So now let's ponder that fantastic word in Romans 5:2—*privilege.*

The context of this verse looks back to what Christ did for us and forward to a glorious future He has promised in our heavenly lives. But now, *right now,* we stand in a place of privilege.

Do we know what we have been given?

I believe when Scripture encourages us to always be ready to explain the hope we have, it is not only for the sake of those who don't know the hope Christ brings to people but it is also for our own sake and the sake of our brothers and sisters in Christ. Know the hope, know the promises, know the riches and treasure. The more we understand the hope and privilege we've been given as children of God, the more we can actually live it.

When our hope knows this place of privilege where we now stand, our perspective of the life we're living is transformed.

✒ BEYOND IMAGINING. ✒
WE'LL JUST HAVE TO LIVE IT

No eye has seen, no ear has heard, and no mind has imagined what God has prepared for those who love him.
— from 1 CORINTHIANS 2:9 —

So how can we describe this place of privilege? What are the "riches" of our inheritance?

I had been a Christian for a long time, yet I wasn't certain I could explain my hope—I wasn't even sure I knew exactly what hope I had as a Christian, beyond the hope of a heavenly life after earthly death. That's why I went searching.

We do have a rich inheritance that covers our past, our present, and our future. This inheritance is God's gift to His children.

This book has focused on how God deals with our past and gives us new life. Another book in the Hope Knows series focuses entirely on the present and how God supplies what we need to live through and deal with today. Yet one more book will look at God's plans for us in the future. Past, present, future—He has given us hope for every part of our lives!

God's plans, though, are far beyond anything we can imagine. The apostle Paul, who saw a great deal of God's power at work, declares that God's mighty power working in our lives can accomplish "infinitely more than we might ask or think" (Ephesians 3:20). That's a promise for our past, for today, and for tomorrow.

I'm okay with that. I'm okay with God bringing more to my life than I would ever imagine. He's already gone beyond my expectations so often that now I'm looking forward with anticipation, eager to see what my Father has planned.

It's my belief that we children of God will live our entire lives here on earth and never exhaust the "deep pockets" of wealth God has for us. And I also suspect we'll discover that our place of privilege has no earthly limits.

ALL THE GOOD THINGS THAT HAVE COME

So Christ has now become the High Priest over all the good things that have come.
- from HEBREWS 9:11 -

Don't let the word *inheritance* mislead you.

I know it carries the idea of "maybe something, sometime." That's the way worldly inheritance works. We wait for something that might be given to us in the future—and sometimes that long-awaited inheritance evaporates before it does actually become ours.

But in the kingdom of God, your inheritance is given to you now, as soon as you become His child. Just as your new, forever-alive life has already begun, so have the benefits of your inheritance. Yes, the greatest, most fantastic part is still to come. There is the promise of a priceless inheritance reserved for us in heaven. But you also have access to your *privilege* of inheritance now.

Look at these Scriptures. And (here comes the grammar teacher again) note the tense of the verbs. These are things that have happened and are happening *now*. They are not referring only to the future:

> The wonderful things God **has** freely **given** us. (1 Corinthians 2:12)
>
> Christ **brought** us into this place of undeserved privilege where we **now stand.** (Romans 5:2)
>
> We **have received** an inheritance from God. (Ephesians 1:11)
>
> He **seated** us in the heavenly realms with Christ. (Ephesians 2:6)
>
> Both Jews and Gentiles **share** equally in the riches. (Ephesians 3:6)
>
> The endless treasure **available** to [those] in Christ. (Ephesians 3:8)

So Christ has now become the High Priest over all the good things **that have come.** (Hebrews 9:11).

(Okay, I admit that not all those words I emphasized are verbs. If you caught that, you get an A in grammar today.)

Our hope is not just for some future reward. *Right now,* God is making all things new for those who come to Him. He has dealt with our past, and the Spirit of Christ leads us into all those new, good things. *Right now.* The promises and hope Christians have are not only for some distant future. They're also bridges we can trust to carry us *right now,* through this very day, and on into an unending future.

Here, again, we see that it all depends on Jesus Christ. He is the one who frees prisoners. He is the high priest who opens the way to the Father. He is the one who makes it possible for us to move from our old life to a new way of life.

Jesus is the one who brings our heavenly inheritance into our living today.

⊱ TO ENTER OR NOT TO ENTER? ⊰
THAT IS THE QUESTION

Look at the inheritance God has put in front of you. Go
forward, take it. Live in the promises. Don't let fear hold
you back, because the bridges of hope to take you forward
are strong and reliable. Haven't they always held you? God
keeps His word. Don't give in to discouragement.

— **DEUTERONOMY 1:21** AP —

The children of Israel had escaped slavery in
Egypt and followed Moses through the wilderness.
They were living on the promise that God was
taking them to a wonderful land they could claim as
their own, a place of great abundance and blessing.

When they finally stood at the borders
of that Promised Land, Moses gave them the
encouraging words in Deuteronomy 1:21 that I
paraphrased above.

Yet the Israelites thought they should be smart
and practical about it—check things out, assess
the situation, conduct a survey, take a vote. *Let's*
see what's ahead of us, they thought, *figure out*
the best way to attack what lies ahead. Let's be
realistic about what's possible.

So they sent twelve spies ahead to survey the
situation. Ten out of twelve—a clear majority—
came back and advised against trying to move
into the land. *It's foolishness,* they said. *Can't*
be done. Those ten seemed to be the ones with

level heads on their shoulders, and their reports discouraged the entire nation.

The two spies in the minority urged going forward with God's plans. They were voted down. But in the end, they were the only ones who God said, "obeyed me wholeheartedly." And they were the only two who were given their own acreage in the land of promise.

Everyone else? They had a glimpse of the land. They were within shouting distance of it. But they never ventured forward on God's promise. They wandered in the desert for the remainder of their lives. Attacked, often hungry and thirsty, sometimes staying close to God and sometimes turning their backs on Him, disciplined by God with terrible things like plagues and fire, with only brief moments of worship and repentance. That was their life.

They never came to live in the inheritance God had promised.

How different it might have been if they had only heeded Moses' encouragement: "Go, and live in your inheritance. You will meet scary things, but don't be afraid. Don't be discouraged. Hasn't God always kept His promises? Hasn't He always watched over you? Hasn't He always been with you and provided for you?" (see Deuteronomy 2:7)

You know where I'm going with this. You

know what I'm going to say next—

This is our story, too. And we have the same choice in front of us.

We have come a long way in the pages of this book—from realizing that Christ came to rescue us from the prisons of darkness, to hearing God's promises that we are in perfect standing with Him and He is giving us a new life and great privileges. Now we are faced with a decision.

For a long time now, God has had plans for His children. Before we were even born, He had a plan to deal with our past. He frees us from the prisons of the past so that we can go ahead and move toward the inheritance He assures us is ours. The bridge of hope is right there at our feet. Our faith only needs to take one step at a time to move across it.

Yes, there will be scary times. Our Father tells us not to be afraid. There will be hard times, but He promises that He will be with us every step of the way, providing what we need.

I hope our story is more like Abraham's, who was called to pull up his tents and move on because God had a better place for him. Like him, we're called to pull up our tents and move on because God has an inheritance He wants to give us—even though, like Abraham, we don't know where we're going!

How scary is that? Well, I guess it all depends on who you decide to trust.

Even when [Abraham] reached the land God had for him, "he lived there by faith— for he was like a foreigner... confidently looking forward to a city with eternal foundations, a city designed and built by God." (from Hebrews 11:9-10)

May Abraham's story be ours, children of God. May we be willing to pull up our tents and move forward over bridges of hope because we have a promise and we trust the One who made it. May we live in our new life and new inheritance now, and still look forward to even greater things planned for us.

For more assurance of the promised inheritance, see the appendix for a list of additional Scriptures.

APPENDIX

 ADDITIONAL SCRIPTURES
FOR STUDY AND ENCOURAGEMENT

We travel many roads in life, and there is not a one that God ignored or forgot or did not know about when He planned bridges of promise to help us along the way.

Then He generously gave us His Word, letting us know what He will do for His people, so that we will be encouraged and confident in our journey.

If you want more comfort and assurance of each section's specific hope, here are more Scriptures. The lists are not complete; you'll find hope on every page of Scripture if you ask God to show it to you. But here's a starting point.

FREEDOM FOR PRISONERS

Psalm 34:4-5; Psalm 68:6; Psalm 77:14; Psalm
96:2; Psalm 102:18-20; Psalm 107:10-16; Psalm
116:16; Psalm 142:6a, 7a; Psalm 146:7; Isaiah
9:4; Isaiah 42:7; Isaiah 61:1; Mark 10:45; Luke
4:18; John 8:31-36; Romans 8:2; Galatians 1:4;
Galatians 3:21-22; Galatians 4:5; Ephesians 1:6-
7; Colossians 1:13-14; 1 Timothy 2:5-6; Titus
2:14; Hebrews 2:14-16; 1 Peter 1:9; 1 Peter 1:18-
20; Revelation 5:9.

FREE FROM THE PENALTY

Psalm 103:10-12; Psalm 107:10,14-15; Psalm 130:7;
Isaiah 43:25; Isaiah 53:5-6, 10-11; Luke 24:47;
John 3:17-19; John 5:24; Acts 10:36; Acts 13:38-
39; Romans 3:23-26; Romans 4:4-6, 16-25; Romans
5:6, 8, 9, 14-19; Romans 8:1, 33-34; 1 Corinthians
1:2, 30; 1 Corinthians 6:11; 2 Corinthians 5:18-
21; Galatians 3:13; Ephesians 2:1-5, 8; Colossians
1:13-14; Colossians 1:19-22; 1 Thessalonians 1:10;
5:9-10; 1 Timothy 2:5-6; Titus 3:3-7; Hebrews
2:16-18; Hebrews 7:22-25; Hebrews 9:11-15, 28;
Hebrews 10:10-18; Hebrews 12:24; 1 Peter 1:18-
19; 2:24; 1 John 2:1-2; Jude 1:24.

FREE TO LIVE A NEW WAY

Mark 14:23-24; Luke 22:20; John 8:31-36; Romans 3:20-24, 30; Romans 4:1-3, 16-25; Romans 4:4-8; Romans 6:14; Romans 7:6; Romans 8:1-4; Romans 8:34; Romans 10:1-4; Galatians 2:16; Galatians 3:5-14, 21-25; Galatians 4:4-7; Galatians 5:1; Ephesians 2:8-9; 1 Timothy 2:5-6; Hebrews 7:19, 22-27; Hebrews 9:13-15, 26-28; Hebrews 10:8-18, 19-23; 1 John 2:1-2. (Yes, might as well read all of Romans, Galatians, and Hebrews!)

FREE FROM MY OLD SELF

Mark 8:34; Luke 9:23; Luke 14:27; Romans 6:3-4, 6-14; Romans 7:21-25; Romans 8:1-4, 7-17; 2 Corinthians 5:14-15; Galatians 2:20; Galatians 3:27; Galatians 5:16-25; Ephesians 1:19-20; Colossians 1:9-14; Colossians 2:11-12; Colossians 3:1-3, 10; Titus 2:14.

NEW LIFE

John 1:12-13; John 3:3, 5-8, 36; John 11:25; Romans 5:18; Romans 6:4; 1 Corinthians 15:20-22, 50; 2 Corinthians 3:6; 2 Corinthians 5:17; Ephesians 1:3; Ephesians 2:1-6; Colossians 2:12-14; Colossians 3:1-11; Titus 3:3-7; 1 Peter 1:3,23.

NEW ACCESS TO GOD

Matthew 27:50-52; Mark 15:37-38; Romans 4:25; Romans 5:6-11, 18; Ephesians 1:4; Ephesians 2:12-13, 17-18; Ephesians 3:12; Colossians 1:19-23; 1 Thessalonians 5:23-24; Hebrews 4:14-16; Hebrews 6:18-20; Hebrews 7:19-28; Hebrews 10:19-23; James 4:8; 1 John 5:20; Jude 1:24.

NEW STATUS

Deuteronomy 4:20; Isaiah 49:6; Matthew 8:11; John 1:10-13; John 11:51-52; Romans 8:14-17, 29-30; Galatians 3:14, 26-29; Galatians 4:4-7; Ephesians 1:5-6, 13-14; Ephesians 2:19-22; Ephesians 3:6; Hebrews 2:10-11; James 1:18; 1 John 3:1-2; 1 John 5:1, 19; Revelation 21:7.

NEW CONNECTION TO GOD

John 14:15-26; John 16:5-15; Acts 5:32; Romans 5:5; Romans 8:10-11 and 15-17; 1 Corinthians 2:9-12; 1 Corinthians 3:16; 1 Corinthians 6:19-20; 2 Corinthians 1:21-22; 2 Corinthians 5:4-5; Galatians 4:4-7; Ephesians 1:13-14,17; Titus 3:5-6; James 1:18; 1 John 2:20; 1 John 2:27; 1 John 3:24; 1 John 4:13, 15; 1 John 5:20.

NEW HEART, NEW CREATION

Psalm 51:10; Jeremiah 24:7; 32:38-39; Ezekiel 36:25-27; Romans 2:28-29; Romans 12:1-2; 2 Corinthians 3:18; 2 Corinthians 5:17; Galatians 2:20; Galatians 3:26-27; Galatians 5:16-26; Galatians 6:15-16; Ephesians 2:10; Ephesians 4:21-24; Ephesians 5:8-9; Philippians 1:6, 11; Philippians 2:13; Colossians 1:27; Colossians 3:1-15; Titus 2:14; Titus 3:4-5; Peter 1:3-4.

NEW REALM OF LIVING

Exodus 19:3-6; Isaiah 8:11-14; Matthew 5:1-12; Mark 1:14-15; Luke 17:20; John 15:18-21; John 16:33; John 17:13-19; John 18:31-36; 1 Corinthians 6:9-11; 2 Corinthians 4:18; 2 Corinthians 5:14-15; Ephesians 2:6, 19; Ephesians 5:6-9; Philippians 3:20; Colossians 1:11-13; Colossians 3:1-15; 1 Timothy 6:17-19; 2 Timothy 3:12; Hebrews 7:25; Hebrews 11:27; Hebrews 12:18-28; 1 Peter 1:17-23; 1 Peter 2:9-11.

NEW POWER FOR LIVING

Psalm 105:4; Isaiah 40:29-31; John 14:15-17; John 14:25-26; John 15:4-5, 26; John 16:13; Acts 1:8; Acts 2:38-39; Romans 6:6-7, 10; Romans 7:6; Romans 8:1-16, 26; 1 Corinthians 2:10-12; 1 Corinthians 4:20; 2 Corinthians 4:7; 2 Corinthians 5:14,17; 2 Corinthians 12:7-10; Galatians 2:20; Galatians 5:16-25; Ephesians 1:19,20; Ephesians 3:16-20; Ephesians 6:10,11,13; Philippians 1:9-11; Philippians 2:13; Philippians 3:10; Philippians 4:13; Colossians 1:11; Titus 3:4-6; Hebrews 13:20-21; 2 Peter 1:3-9.

NEW LIFE EXPECTANCY

Deuteronomy 30:19-20; Isaiah 51:6; Matthew 25:46; John 3:14-17; John 3:36; John 5:24,26; John 6:35-40, 47-51, 57-58, 68; John 11:25-26; John 17:2-3; John 20:30-31; Romans 5:21; Romans 6:23; 2 Corinthians 4:16-18; 2 Corinthians 5:1; Galatians 6:8; 1 Thessalonians 4:13-14,17-18; 2 Timothy 1:9-10; Titus 1:1-2; Titus 3:7-8; Hebrews 2:14-15; Hebrews 5:8-9; 1 Peter 1:20, 23-25; 1 John 2:17, 24-25; 1 John 5:10-13, 20.

NEW IDENTITY AND PURPOSE

New identity: Exodus 19:4-6; Deuteronomy 4:20; Deuteronomy 7:6; Deuteronomy 10:14-15; Isaiah 43:7, 10, 21; Acts 26:17-18; Romans 1:6-7; Galatians 3:14, 29; Ephesians 1:14; Titus 2:14; 1 Peter 2:9-10.

Words to God's holy people: Luke 6:35-36; John 17:15-17; Romans 1:6-7; Romans 15:16; 1 Corinthians 1:2; 1 Corinthians 1:30-31; 1 Corinthians 6:11; Ephesians 4:1, 20-24; Colossians 1:22; Colossians 3:12; 1 Thessalonians 4:7-8; 5:23-24; 2 Thessalonians 1:11-12; 2 Timothy 1:9; Hebrews 2:11; Hebrews 10:14; Hebrews 12:10; 1 Peter 2:9; 2 Peter 3:11-14.

Words for the inadequate and unqualified: John 14:17, 20, 23; John 15:4-5; John 17:23; Romans 8:10-11; 1 Corinthians 6:19; 2 Corinthians 4:6-7; 2 Corinthians 12:9; Galatians 2:20; Ephesians 3:17; Philippians 1:11; Colossians 1:27; Hebrews 13:21.

Words to the Temple of God: 1 Corinthians 3:9, 16; 2 Corinthians 6:16; Ephesians 2:19-22; Hebrews 3:6; 1 Peter 2:4-5.

Words to those entrusted with the message: Matthew 28:18-20; Mark 16:15; Luke 24:47; John 17:18; 1 Corinthians 10:31; 2 Corinthians 3:6; 2 Corinthians 5:18-21; Colossians 3:17; Hebrews 3:1; 1 Peter 2:11-12; 1 Peter 4:11; Jude 1:3.

NEW INHERITANCE

Deuteronomy 1:21; Psalm 61:5; Matthew 25:34; Acts 20:32; Romans 5:1-2; Romans 8:15-17, 23; 1 Corinthians 2:7-12; Galatians 3:6-9, 26, 29; Galatians 4:7; Ephesians 1:11, 13-14; Ephesians 2:6; Ephesians 3:6, 8; Colossians 1:12; Hebrews 9:11-15, 28; 1 Peter 1:4; Revelation 21:7.